Press Breakers

Bob Huggins

ISBN: 1-58518-360-1
Library of Congress Control Number: 00-108326
Front cover photo: Bob Rosato
Cover design: Jennifer Boklemann
Text design and diagrams: Jeanne Hamilton

Printed in the United States of America

Coaches Choice
P. O. Box 1828
Monterey, CA 93942
www.coacheschoice.com
Fax: (831) 372-6075
Tel: (831) 372-6077

CONTENTS

A difficulty frequently faced by many coaches in today's game is getting their players to react in a positive, poised, controlled, and aggressive manner to the variety of pressure defenses they will face. Many defensive coaches will employ full-court, three-quarter court, man-to-man, zone, or combination presses to test the preparedness of their team to deal with pressure. Every year, at some point in the season, you know that you're going to play a team that depends on its pressure being better than your press offense. Other teams will have their press ready simply to test if you're prepared. If you are, they quickly get out of it, and if not, the pressure increases as their confidence grows.

You can give your players a sequence of sound options. You can drill them on being strong with the ball on double-teams so they develop tremendous confidence in their ability to handle pressure.

The objective of the *press breakers* is to advance the ball across the center line and create high-percentage scoring opportunities at the offensive end of the floor. A team that is content to simply break the pressure and stop once they have the ball over half-court doesn't make the defense pay, eliminating any risk they are taking by extending and pressuring. As an offensive team, you must take advantage of an over-extended defense by getting into your offense before the defense completely recovers. For a press offense to be consistently successful, it must understand and attack a defense that places itself in this tenuous situation.

This book includes set plays that will enable you to use your players' individual talents, while still staying within a team concept. These sets provide focus for every position so that you can:

- Play to your team's strengths

- Exploit the opponent's weaknesses

- Create desired matchups

- Isolate poor defenders to score or create fouls

- Keep the ball in the hands of your better ball handlers

- Position your players where they are most effective

To accomplish the above objectives, Chapter 1 offers nine drills designed to develop each individual's ability to attack pressure, both mentally and physically. You can use these drills to cultivate your own players' ability to handle pressure whether you intend to use the press breakers or not.

Chapter 2 describes in detail what is expected from each position while running the press breakers.

Chapter 3 introduces the 1-up press breaker series. It's called 1-up because only one player is stationed near the man throwing the ball inbounds. Two attackers are stationed near midcourt, and the final player is at the opposite free-throw line. This eight-sequence progression may be all you'll ever need to break any press.

Chapter 4 outlines breakdown drills that teach the 1-up press breaker. You can use these drills to work on that portion of the press which is giving you the most trouble, or to teach the entire 1-up press breaker program.

Chapter 5 explains how the 1-up press breaker works its magic against the three major presses: the box-and-one (2-2-1), the diamond-and-one (1-2-1-1), and the various man-to-man tactics. When you're through with this chapter, you'll have a full-fledged strategy of teaching and attacking presses.

Chapter 6 describes the 2-up press breaker series. You can use the 2-up press breaker as a change-up to the 1-up. It's exactly like the 1-up series except you bring a second player up to help get the ball inbounds. This is frequently used against face guard or denial presses, whether man-to-man or zone.

Chapter 7 provides breakdown drills to teach the 2-up series.

Chapter 8 describes bringing up a third player, so it's logically called the 3-up series.

Chapter 9 presents breakdown drills to teach the 3-up series.

Chapter 10 outlines the 4-up press breaker patterns. This means you begin with four players near the inbound passer; you still run the same sequence of moves. The 4-up press breaker, as well as the 2-up and 3-up, is easy to learn once the 1-up program has been mastered.

Chapter 11 presents the breakdown drills used to teach the fundamentals of the 4-up series.

You can use the 1-, 2-, 3-, and 4-up maneuvers interchangeably, or you can use any one of the programs as your entire press offense for the year. You can exchange one for another anywhere in the game to keep your opponents off guard.

Chapter 12 describes the advantages of fast breaking to the basket once you get the ball to half-court. This makes opponents pay for the extension of their defenses. It also includes the secondary phase of attack, just before you get into your motion offense.

Chapter 13 describes the beauty of the fast-break attack expanded to combat half-court zone presses. If you can use the same ideas to attack half-court traps, you have less to teach, and your players will be able to execute your offenses better.

Over the years these plays have been very effective for us in attempting to get the most out of our personnel. Naturally, you can rely on your better players, identifying what they can or cannot do every year, but you can also try to make each player better with these drills as the season progresses.

Let's go beat those presses!

KEY

1 2 3 4 5	OFFENSIVE PLAYERS
X1 X2 X3 X4 X5	DEFENSIVE PLAYERS
——————→	CUT
→▶▶▶▶▶▶	PASS
∿∿∿→	DRIBBLE
——————⊣	SCREEN

CHAPTER 1

Press Breaker Individual Drills

This chapter presents nine individual drills designed to improve, physically and mentally, even your worst ball handler. Each drill includes a figure, procedures, and objectives (things you want your players to get out of the drill). By practicing these drills early in the season, your team will develop the poise and control necessary to defeat pressure teams.

Each drill requires a minimum of personnel, which maximizes the repetitions in a given amount of time and allows you to quickly spot and correct flawed fundamentals. These drills also have the benefit of compelling intensity and concentration. Flawed fundamentals have a way of showing up very quickly, giving you an opportunity to work on improving them early in the year, developing your players to their fullest potential.

1-ON-1 ZIGZAG DRILL

Any player who receives the ball in open court may have to beat his defender in a 1-on-1 dribbling move. That's the major purpose of this drill: to build confidence in the dribbler so he feels he can beat any defender — at least for a few dribbles.

Procedure:

- Line up players as shown in Figure 1-1.
- Let an offensive player have the basketball. This player is to dribble down the floor and back again before exchanging places with the defender.
- The original defender then dribbles down the floor and back.
- The coach can require as many trips down the floor and back as needed to develop the players' ability to attack a lone defender in open court.
- The coach can limit the dribbler to only one move (spin, half-spin, crossover, in-and-out, etc.), or the coach can permit two, three, four, or more moves.
- Divide the court into thirds. The boundaries are the sidelines and the free-throw lane lines extended all the way down the floor.
- Put your better ball handlers and quicker defenders in the middle lane because it has a smaller area. The dribbler must stay inside his third of the court all the way down and back.
- Defenders must turn the dribbler (make the attacker change directions) three times in each half-court.
- You can begin by having the dribbler walk the ball up the court and progress to full speed. Once you start full-speed drills, the defender must race to catch up to the dribbler when passed.

Objectives:

- To teach the ball handler to dribble out of pressure.
- To teach basic offensive dribbling moves and fundamentals.
- To teach defenders to pressure the ball without losing the dribbler.
- To teach a post player respect for a guard. When you have a post player who gets angry with a quicker guard for *hogging* the show, just put the post player in the middle lane versus that same guard. The post player will quickly gain great respect for the guard, and become a better player for it.

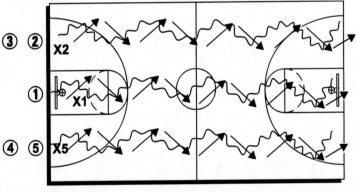

Figure 1-1

2-ON-1 STEP-THROUGH

Sometime during each player's career he'll be double-teamed. This drill is designed to help that double-teamed player escape with a simple step-through move. The player fakes in one direction, then swings the ball very low (around ankle top) and very quickly in between himself and his defender. Now he can toss the ball out in front and go get it, continuing his dribble. The ball must be out of the dribbler's hand before he picks up his pivot foot.

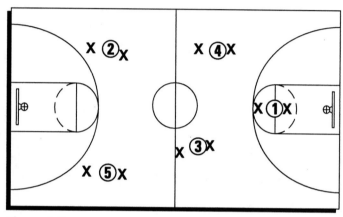

Figure 1-2

Procedure:

- Line up players as shown in Figure 1-2: two defenders and the dribbler. After 30 seconds, one of the defenders becomes the new dribbler while the original dribbler becomes one of the defenders. After another 30 seconds, the player who has not been the dribbler yet rotates to that position while the other two become the new defenders.

- The ball handler pivots as long as he can, keeping the ball out of the reach of either defender.

- Defenders are allowed to slap at the ball, even hitting arms if they so desire.

- After pivoting for several seconds, keeping the ball from being slapped away, the dribbler fakes in one direction before coming back and splitting the defenders. Once he splits the defenders, the dribbler tosses the ball out in front of him, goes to get the ball, touching it with only one hand, and commences a dribble.

- Defenders can trail this dribble, trying to flick the ball away.

- The dribbler can fake one direction, then drive around the other defender as a last resort.

Objectives:

- To teach a player who is double-teamed to control the ball.

- To teach the dribbler to pivot, keeping the ball from being exposed to either defender.

- To teach the dribbler to split the defenders by faking in one direction, then coming back for the split. The dribbler must get both defenders in motion by using his pivots before he tries the step-through move.

- To teach the dribbler to blast away from the trap once he has been successful with his step-through move.

- To teach the dribbler to drive around one side of the defenders if he's not successful with the step-through move.

2-ON-1 ESCAPE

Good ball handlers can escape even two defenders and bring the ball down the court. These ball handlers not only employ the step-through move, but also use the retreat dribble before blasting around one side or the other of two defenders. That is the major purpose of this drill.

Procedure:

- Line up players as shown in Figure 1-3. Each set of three can use only half the court. (An imaginary line goes from basket to basket. The dribbler must stay inside this imaginary line and the sidelines.)

- Figure 1-3 illustrates a coach passing to O1 in the corner but inside the three-point line. It also illustrates defender X1 underneath the basket and defender X3 where the sideline meets the free-throw line if it were extended. This simulates the diamond-and-one press. Make sure the next time you do this drill, the ball handler and the defenders start at different positions on the court.

- O1 begins his dribble trying to escape the double-team of the two defenders. O1 can drive to the middle, as if he's going to split the defenders, then use a quick-retreat dribble, fake one direction, then drive around the defenders in the other direction.

- The two defenders trap again if they can catch the dribbler before he reaches the other baseline.

- The dribbler must stay in his half of the court. During the game, the dribbler would have the full-court, but this limitation in the drill makes it harder for the dribbler to escape the double team.

- After O1 has dribbled to near midcourt, the coach passes to O2 for the same action to occur on the other half of the court.

- After the players go to the other baseline, the coach goes to that end and lets the players stay where they are for a trip back down the floor. Then they rotate. After the first rotation, the players go down the floor and back before the second rotation. After the second rotation, all three players should have been on offense.

Objectives:

- To teach the dribbler to escape a double-team by use of the retreat dribble, change of pace, and change of direction.

- To teach defenders to set good double-team traps.

- To teach the dribbler good ball control, poise and confidence.

- To condition.

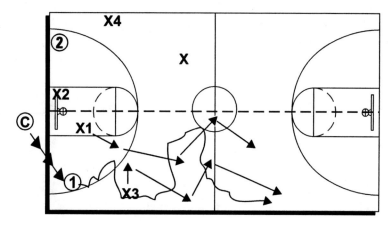

Figure 1-3

3-ON-1 PASSING

Every player on your team will at some time need to make a decision about where to pass the ball against pressure. He will also need to decide whether to fake pass before passing in another direction. This drill develops confidence in making the correct pass at the proper moment.

Procedure:

- Line up players as shown in Figure 1-4.

- O1 has the ball and is to pass to either O2 or O3, who should be spaced about

15 feet apart. X1 should be between and slightly in front of the two receivers, down and ready to attempt an interception, or at least a deflection. As coach, you can require O1 to make a bounce pass, a chest pass, or a flip-lob pass, or you can leave that decision to O1.

- O1 can fake passing in one direction before passing in the other. Or, O1 can fake one pass, such as a bounce pass, before making a different pass.

- Should O1 be successful, let's say to O2, then X1 moves over to cover between O1 and O3.

- This continues until X1 gets at least one deflection. Then the passer who threw the deflection (or interception) takes X1's place while X1 takes his.

Objectives:

- To teach poise and control while passing against full-court pressure. (Figure 1-4 illustrates the player positions for a pass from the corner to the free-throw line or to the free-throw line extended. Move these positions when you use this drill again. You can simulate actual pressing angles each time you change the spots.)

- To teach fake passing.

- To teach accurate passing.

- To teach the defender proper angles to play when pressing.

- To teach the defender to read the passer's body language, including stance and visual cues.

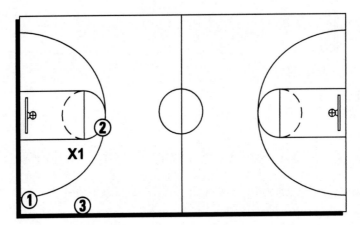

Figure 1-4

3-ON-3 CONTINUOUS TRAPPING

This continuous trapping and passing drill teaches all the fundamentals of the first four drills simultaneously.

Procedure:

- Line up players as shown in Figure 1-5.

- On any deflection or interception, the offense rotates to the defense and the defense becomes the offense.

- The receiver may immediately pass on any reception, or he may catch the ball, fake pass in one direction, then pass in another direction.

- The receiver may fake a step in one direction, then use the step-through move to split the defenders.

- After several rounds of this drill, the coach may allow a dribble of two or three steps before the dribbler picks up the ball. All dribblers and defenders move the same two or three steps in that direction before reapplying the trapping and interception spots. This helps teach the step-through and the retreat dribble to try to escape the double-team.

Objectives:

- To teach proper trapping techniques.
- To teach proper interception angles.
- To teach fake passing.
- To teach touch passing.
- To teach awareness of a player's peripheral vision.

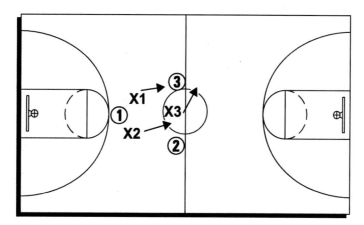

Figure 1-5

- To teach the retreat dribble.
- To teach the step-through move.
- To teach aggressive offensive and defensive play.
- To teach poise and control under pressure defenses.

TRAP AND UMBRELLA DRILL

This drill will help players recognize defensive alignments. All traps and interception angles, regardless of whether they begin as the box-and-one, the diamond-and-one, or man-to-man tactics, take the form of two players on the ball trapping the ball handler, and two players in the interception spots against three potential outlet receivers (the umbrella). This occurs all over the court, so it is important to allow each player a chance to play the O2 spot in Figure 1-6.

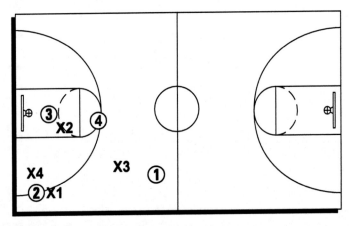

Figure 1-6

Procedure:

- Line up players as shown in Figure 1-6.
- O2 has the ball, and he has three potential receivers, as any good press offense will give him. O1 has the spot near the sideline, O4 has the diagonal-cutting spot, and O3 provides the throw-back passing angle.
- X1 and X4 are trapping the ball. X2 and X3 are in the interception spots.
- After several attempted passes, the offense should rotate from O1 to O2 to O3 to O4. This gives every one a chance to play each position.
- When the offense rotates, the defense also rotates from X1 to X2 to X3 to X4.
- After all players have played each position, the offense becomes the defense and the defense becomes the offense.
- Positioning of the players should change from day-to-day.

Objectives:

- To teach the offense to recognize the trap and the umbrella defensive maneuvers.
- To teach ball handlers to fake pass, step-through, and retreat dribble.
- To teach potential receivers to step toward the pass to receive it.
- To teach defenders proper angles for interceptions and traps.

3-ON-4 FULL-COURT TRAPPING

This is an aggressive attacking drill that adds the element of compelling receivers to get open for an outlet pass. It allows the retreating dribble, the fake pass, the step-through, etc., to break the press. Once the offense gains an advantage, it attacks the basket at the far end of the court with an aggressive fast break.

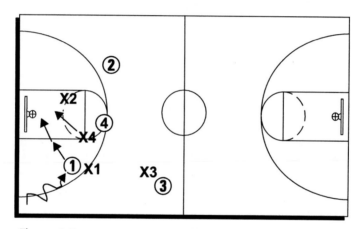

Figure 1-7

Procedure:

- Line up players as shown in Figure 1-7.
- O1 has the ball and is being trapped by X1 and X4. X4 is the designated trapper. He will leave the player with the ball and go trap the new pass receiver. O1 is defended by X1, O2 by X2, and O3 by X3. This continues until O1, O2, and O3 break the press and can fast break to the far end of the court. Then they set up and come back down the court. The defense becomes the new offense, and the offense rotates to defense. Designate one of the old defenders to stay on defense as X4.
- The ball handler may use any technique (retreat dribble, step-through, etc.).
- Receivers are guarded 1-on-1. They must make strategic moves to free themselves for a possible reception.

- In Figure 1-7, O1 is trapped and passes back to O2 who freed himself from X2. X2 immediately goes to cover O2's left side advancement because X2 knows he has help coming from where the ball was, namely X4 coming from that angle. The other two defenders play denial defense on their assignments.

- Once O2 has the ball, he tries to dribble past his two defenders, or to pass to O1 or O3. O1 and O3 must work to get open because X1 and X3 will try to deny them the pass.

- You can make it an even more overloaded situation by removing O3 and X3, making it a 2-on-3 drill.

- This continues until the offense breaks the press and fast breaks.

Objectives:

- To teach the offense to aggressively attack the defense and the basket.

- To teach the offense the proper techniques of retreat dribbling, fake passing, step-through, etc.

- To teach the defense proper angles for interceptions and traps.

TRAP, UMBRELLA, AND SAFETY DRILL

All presses (zone or man-to-man) end in two defenders setting the trap, two defenders covering the three outlet-pass lanes (the umbrella), and a defender located nearer the basket to prevent the lay-up (the safety). These traps and umbrellas can be almost anywhere on the court, but most of the time the defense tries to use the sidelines and the corners as its trapping area. You should practice this drill from different areas of the court from day-to-day. It allows your ball handlers to recognize where their teammates will be in relation to the trapping area. Figure 1-8 illustrates the trap about 28 feet up the left sideline.

Procedure:

- Line up players as shown in Figure 1-8. Rotate offensive players through all five positions. Likewise, rotate defenders from X1 to X5. After each player has played each position, rotate offense and defense and repeat the process.

- In the figure O1 is trapped by X1 and X4. O1 should fake pass, use the step-through, or apply the retreat dribble. O1 should never get near the sideline. He should stay several feet from the sideline so he can use that side of the court to drive by his opponent if need be.

- O1 can turn his back on one side of the court and quickly turn back. Defenders X2 and X3 should react by moving quickly in the direction O1 turns to pass the ball. This allows the umbrella defenders, X2 and X3, to cover all three outlet-pass lanes. Of course, when actually playing a game, you don't want O1 to turn his back. He should always square up first so he can see all potential pass receivers down the floor.

- X5 should cheat up toward the umbrella for a possible lob-pass interception. O1 must be aware of this.

- Allow O1 to make several passes to the up players: O2, O3, and O4.

- Allow O1 to make several passes to the deep attacker, O5, who should cut to get open and keep X5 busy.

Objectives:

- To allow O1 to see how a press always looks, regardless of whether it's man-to-man or zone. This teaches poise and control under pressure.

- To teach O1 to make the correct choice of passes.

- To teach O1 to retreat dribble, step-through, or fake before passing.

- To teach the trappers proper methods of trapping.

- To teach defenders proper angles to make interceptions and deflections.

- To teach the safety of the press how to play that position.

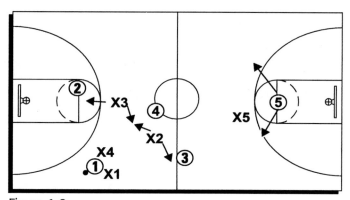

Figure 1-8

POST, PIVOT, PASS, AND BREAK

The goal of breaking the press is to get the lay-up or a good shot on the other end of the court. In other words, make the opponents pay for extending their defense. A team that's content to just get the ball over half-court, then set up their offense, will be pressed, pressed, and pressed at no peril to the defense. Hence, this drill shows how to break to the three outlet-pass positions, quickly make a pass of a reception, and fast break to the other end of the court. Change the starting position from practice to practice.

Procedure:

- Line up players as shown in Figure 1-9.

- O3 is not trapped, nor does O3 take part in the fast break. This allows O3 to easily find his open teammates, O1, O2, or O4, who are cutting to the three outlet positions against the umbrella.

- O3 can fake pass in one direction, then pass in another; simulate a step-through, then pass; or alter his position on the court by retreat dribbling and driving around the imaginary defenders for a step or two. This requires O1, O2, and O4 to adjust their angles.

- Figure 1-9 illustrates O3 passing to the posting O4, who pivots and passes to O1 racing down the side lane. O1 receives this pass and dribbles the ball to the center lane. O4 fills the outside lane. O1 fills the other side lane. The two defenders retreat quickly to make it a 3-on-2 fast break.

- O3 does not have to pass to O4; he can pass to either O2 or O1. Use your press offensive cuts regardless of whom O3 passes to.

Objectives:

- To teach O3 to recognize the umbrella and make the correct pass.
- To teach O1, O2, and 4 to cut to get open.
- To teach the cuts of your press offense regardless of where the ball is initially passed.
- To teach fast breaking once your team has broken the press.
- To condition.

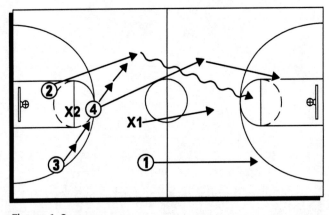

Figure 1-9

Summary

If you adjust these drills to teach the cuts you've chosen for a press breaker, then the drills will teach your press philosophy as your players are learning the fundamentals of press breaking.

Now that you have a sound foundation to build your attack against a press, let's move on to the press breaker.

CHAPTER 2

Characteristics and Responsibilities for Each Press Breaker Position

This chapter defines the characteristics and responsibilities needed to fill the press breaker positions. O3 will be the inbounder. O2 will be the primary up-man. O1 will be the ballside half-court man; he is also the point guard. O4 will be the opposite side half-court man. And O5 will be the back-man. These numbers are used consistently throughout the next 12 chapters, always representing the same positions.

Offensively, O2 will be the shooting guard, O3 the shooting forward, O4 the power forward, and O5 the post player. You may have to make some adjustments to fit your personnel. You will have enough latitude so that someone on your squad will have the features to fill each and every position. And where they are a little deficient, use the drills in the first chapter to develop those skills.

Inbounder

Characteristics:

- Average to better than average decision maker.
- Average to better than average passer.

- Average to better than average ball handler.
- Ability to see the whole floor.
- Ability to put good velocity on cross-court passes.
- Good arms a plus.

Responsibilities:

- Takes the ball out from any point on the baseline except directly under the basket.
- Gets the ball inbounded.
- Understands and can read his four options:
  - ❑ Deep man
  - ❑ Primary up-man
  - ❑ Ballside half-court man
  - ❑ Opposite side half-court man
- Inbounds the ball to the correct man at the proper time.
- Stays behind the ball as an outlet after inbounding.
- Maintains a 15 to 17 foot space away from and behind the ball.
- Reverses the ball quickly from one side of the floor to the other.
- Continues to stay behind the ball creating a passing angle and acting as a safety in case of a turnover.

Primary Up-Man

Characteristics:

- Ability to get open 1-on-1 or even 1-on-2.
- Excellent decision maker under pressure.
- Strong hands with the basketball.
- Ability to attack and defeat double-teams with either a pass or a dribble.
- A high percentage free-throw shooter.
- Size and strength a plus.

Responsibilities:

- Gets open and is the first option of the inbounder.
- Catches the ball inside the three-point arch and outside the first block on the lane so he has room to maneuver and work out of traps (Figure 2-1).
- Immediately squares up when he receives the first pass, not allowing the defense to force him to turn his back on his potential receivers.
- Understands and can read his four options:
    - ❑ Deep man at your basket
    - ❑ Ballside half-court man
    - ❑ Offside half-court man flashing to the middle
    - ❑ Reversing the ball back to the inbounder
- Passes the ball and fills the appropriate lane.

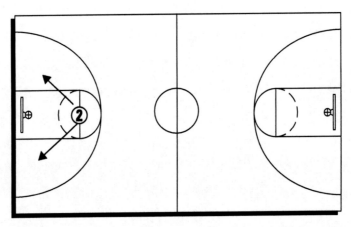

Figure 2-1

Ballside Half-Court Man

Characteristics:

- Usually the best ball handler.
- Best decision maker in the open floor.
- Good passer in transition.
- Adequate speed and quickness.

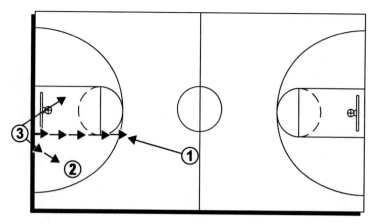

Figure 2-2

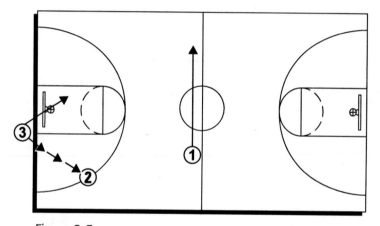

Figure 2-3

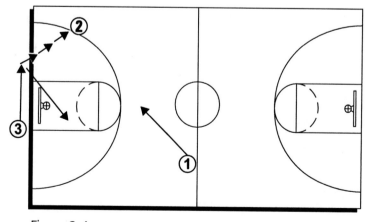

Figure 2-4

Responsibilities:

- Makes himself available to receive the inbounds pass (Figure 2-2).
- Is the first option if the up-man receives the inbounds pass on his side of the floor.
- If covered, quickly crosses the floor and positions himself with his back to the sideline (Figure 2-3).
- If the up-man catches the ball on the opposite side of his initial position, flashes diagonally to the middle of the floor (Figure 2-4).
- Always squares up and faces up the court when he catches the ball.
- Advances the ball up the court with either the pass or the dribble.
- Generally looks to pass the ball to the opposite side from which he came.

Opposite-Side Half-Court Man

Characteristics:

- Presents a big target.
- Ability to catch the ball while coming to meet it.
- Can pivot and make the diagonal pass.
- Good hands.

Responsibilities:

- Makes himself available to receive the inbounds pass if the inbounder runs the baseline in his direction (Figure 2-5).

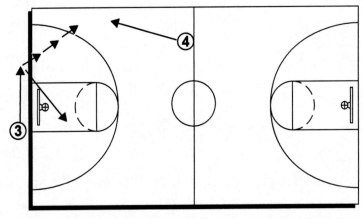

Figure 2-5

- Flashes diagonally to the middle of the floor and presents a big target if the up-man receives the inbounds pass on the opposite side of the floor (Figure 2-6).

- Upon catching the ball, pivots and looks to hit the cross-man diagonally and opposite.

- Is the first option should the up-man catch the entry pass on his side of the floor, but if covered, he must quickly cross the floor and position himself with his back to the sideline (Figure 2-7).

- Looks to receive the ball and advance it.

- Always follows this *key rule:* If the ball is passed same side cross, then the opposite side flashes to the middle. Have the players repeat to themselves, "Same side cross, opposite side middle."

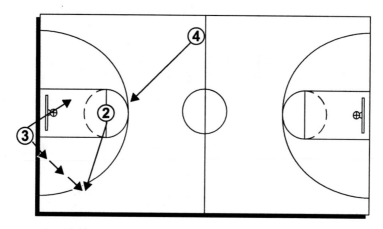

Figure 2-6

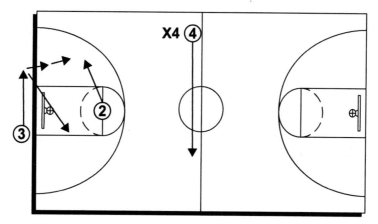

Figure 2-7

Back-Man

Characteristics:

- Best finisher.
- Not necessarily a good ball handler – can be hidden in this position.
- Good offensive rebounder.

Responsibilities:

- Aligns in the middle of the floor at the offensive foul line.
- Always threatens the long pass first (Figure 2-8).
- If the first pass doesn't go to him, reads the second pass to determine his next cut.
- Goes wide to the sideline opposite the direction of the second pass (Figure 2-9).
- If the second pass goes to the middle of the floor, goes to the side opposite of where the pass came from (Figure 2-10).
- As the ball is advanced down the floor, looks to fill the lane and finish in transition.
- Rebounds the weakside on any shot taken in transition.
- If the back-man receives the ball away from the basket, looks to make a return pass to a ball handler in the middle of the court and then fill in on transition.

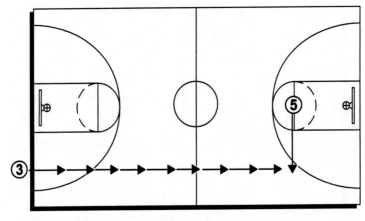

Figure 2-8

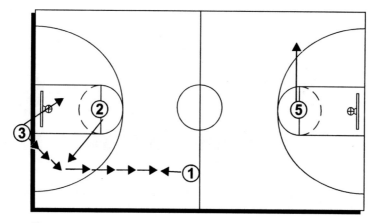

Figure 2-9

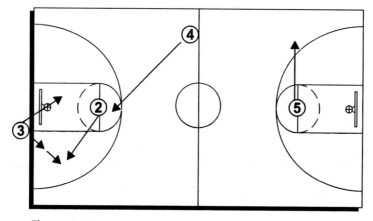

Figure 2-10

Summary

You likely have a player on your team who already has the characteristics to fill each of the five positions. But if you don't, you can build one; just go back to Chapter 1 and do the drills necessary to develop such a player. Even if you have players to fill all the positions, you can improve their fundamentals with the drills in Chapter 1.

Now that you know the characteristics and responsibilities of each position, you're ready to actually begin teaching the cuts and the options. Chapter 3 will explain the eight available options.

1-Up Press Breaker

This chapter outlines eight steps in developing the full press breaker. Under normal defenses, these are the only steps you'll need to have a complete and sound press breaker. This chapter covers in detail how each step works.

STEP ONE

Initial Pass to the Up-Man

The initial pass to the up-man is the option most often used. (See Figure 3-1.)

Player O1:

- Stays on the ballside for a potential pass from O2.
- Quickly crosses the floor getting his back to the sideline and stays wide.
- Follows the rule *same side cross, opposite side middle.*

Player O2:

- Starts in the middle of the floor near the top of the key.
- Uses a change of direction to get open. Catches and squares to see up the floor.
- After receiving the inbounds pass, reads the following:
  - ❏ O5 down the floor
  - ❏ O1 ballside
  - ❏ O4 flashing to the middle
  - ❏ O3 angled behind as the trailer
- Always looks to advance the ball up the floor first.

Player O3:

- Inbounds the ball to O2 and steps inbounds behind the ball for a reversal.
- Creates an easy passing angle for O2 with 15 to 17 feet of spacing.

Player O4:

- Begins at half-court opposite O1.
- Flashes diagonally to the middle looking for a pass from O2 as he squares.
- Comes to meet the ball.
- Follows the rule *same side cross, opposite side middle.*

Player O5:

- Begins on the offensive foul line and waits to read the second pass.

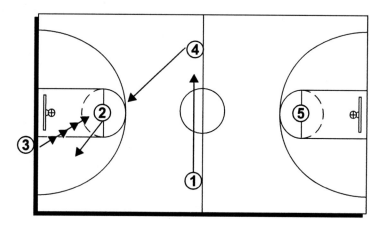

Figure 3-1

STEP TWO

Second Pass to Half-Court Man, Same Side

This step allows the up-man to get the ball and pass to the half-court man on the same side of the court. Then the up-man (O2) makes the diagonal cut that cannot be stopped by a zone press. (See Figure 3-2.)

Player O1:

- Stays on the ballside looking for a pass from O2.

- Comes to meet the pass from O2.

- Catches and squares facing up court; the first look is for O5.

- As a second option, takes the ball to the middle on the dribble as O4 fills the lane.

Player O2:

- Catches, squares, and gives the first look to O5 up the floor opposite.

- Second look is to O1 on the ballside of the court.

- After passing the ball to O1, fills the lane opposite O4 as O1 dribbles to the middle of the floor.

Player O3:

- After passing the ball inbounds, steps in and trails 15 to 17 feet.

- Acts as the safety, preventing any opposition from getting behind him for a lay-up on a turnover or counterbreak.

Player O4:

- Begins at half-court on the opposite side from O1.

- Does not make the diagonal cut to the middle of the floor unless O1 leaves the ballside of the floor.

- Fills the lane when O1 receives the second pass and dribbles to the middle.

Player O5:

- Starts on the offensive foul line and goes to the side opposite the second pass.

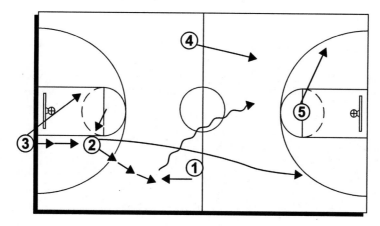

Figure 3-2

STEP THREE

Second Pass to the Middle-Diagonal Cutter

Instead of the up-man passing to the half-court man on the same side of the court, the opposite side half-court man makes the flash-pivot cut to the middle of the court. (See Figure 3-3.)

Player O1:

- Looks for the second pass from O2, but when covered, crosses the court to the sideline in the area that O4 has just vacated.

- Positions himself with his back to the sideline and looks for a pass from O4.

- If he receives the pass from O4, turns and attacks the middle of the floor with the dribble, looking for teammates who are filling the lanes.

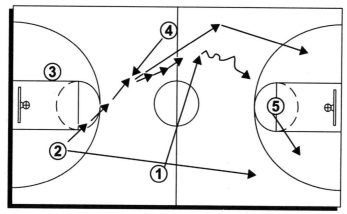

Figure 3-3

Player O2:

- Sees that O5 and O1 are covered up the floor, so passes to O4, flashing diagonally to the middle of the floor.
- Immediately fills the lane on the near side after passing to O4.

Player O3:

- Trails at the correct spacing and angle.
- As the ball is passed to O4, repositions himself to trail and keep spacing for O4.
- Acts as the safety, keeping everyone in front of him.

Player O4:

- Begins on the sideline opposite O1 and flashes to the middle when O1 is covered.
- Receives the pass and squares to make his reads:
  - ❏ O5 deep
  - ❏ O1 diagonally in the area O4 just vacated
  - ❏ O2 filling the lane on the side he just passed from
- If everyone is covered, reverses the ball to O3.

Player O5:

- Waits in his initial position, reads the second pass, and goes to the opposite side.

STEP FOUR

Reverse Back To O3

The up-man passes back to the inbounder, which permits a quick reversal of the ball. (See Figure 3-4.)

Player O1:

- O2 is unable to make the pass to O1 because he's being defended.
- O1 crosses the floor with his back to the opposite sideline and wide.

Player O2:

- Cannot pass to O1 or O4 flashing to the middle, so reverses the ball to O3.

- Fills the lane on his side, staying wide to the sideline, spreading the defense.
- Cuts diagonally to the middle if O4 receives the ball from O3.

Player O3:

- Trails 15 to 17 feet and receives the reverse pass from O2.
- Catches, squares, and looks long to O5 first.
- Second look is to O1, who has crossed to his sideline.
- Next look is to O4 in the middle.
- Wherever he passes the ball, trails and acts as a safety to guard the goal.

Player O4:

- Stays in the middle of the floor after flashing and maintains good spacing.
- If he receives the ball from O3, looks for O5 long, O1 filling the lane, or O2 cutting diagonally to the middle of the floor.

Player O5:

- Reads the second pass from his initial position and reacts opposite.

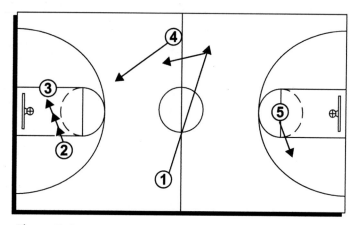

Figure 3-4

STEP FIVE

Inbound Pass Goes to O1

When the up-man (O2) cannot get the inbounds pass, he cuts away from the inbounder. This allows the half-court player on the side of the inbounder (O1) to break back toward the inbounder for the press. (See Figure 3-5.)

Player O1:

- Sees that O2 cannot get open to receive the inbound pass, so he breaks to the ball.
- Catches and squares, looking first to O5 deep.
- Second look is to O2 cutting diagonally to the ballside sideline.
- Next look is to O4 flashing to the middle.
- Last look is to O3 in position to have the ball reversed.

Player O2:

- Is tightly defended and cannot get the inbound pass.
- After O1 receives the pass, makes a diagonal cut in front of O1 toward the sideline.
- If he does not get the ball on the cut, quickly crosses the floor and assumes O1's responsibilities.
- Stays wide on the sideline looking for the ball to be reversed.

Player O3:

- Inbounds the ball, trails for the reversal, and acts as the safety.

Player O4:

- Waits for O2 to clear the middle and then flashes into the middle of the floor.
- If he catches the second pass from O1, then he makes his reads:
  - ❑ O5 deep
  - ❑ O2 on the sideline cut
  - ❑ O3 for a reversal

Player O5:

- Begins on the offensive foul line, reads the second pass, and goes opposite.

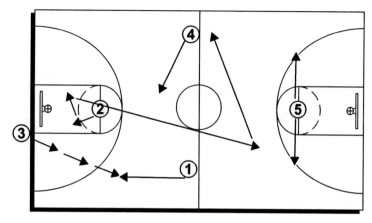

Figure 3-5

STEP SIX

Initial Inbound Pass to O4

When the inbounder cannot get the pass to either the up-man (O2) or the half-court player on the side of the inbounder (O1), the inbounder runs the baseline. When the opposite half-court attacker (O4) sees the inbounder (O3) running the baseline, O4 cuts to get open. (See Figure 3-6.)

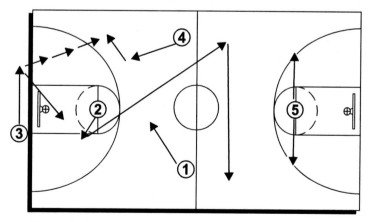

Figure 3-6

Player O1:

- Reads that O3 is running the baseline; waits for O4 to catch the ball and O2 to clear the middle.
- Flashes into the middle of the floor.
- If he receives the ball, then he makes his reads:
  - ❑ O5 deep
  - ❑ Dribbles the ball upcourt
  - ❑ O2 on the sideline cut
  - ❑ O3 for a reversal

Player O2:

- Starts in the middle of the floor and as soon as O4 catches, cuts diagonally in front of O4 to the sideline looking for a pass.
- If he does not get the pass by the time he gets to the near sideline, he quickly crosses the floor and assumes the half-court position on the far side.
- Stays wide on the sideline waiting for the ball to be reversed.

Player O3:

- Runs the baseline toward O4's side of the floor.
- Inbounds the ball to O4 and assumes his trail position and responsibilities.

Player O4:

- Sees that O3 is running the baseline and uses a V-cut and timing to get open.
- If he receives the inbound pass, then he makes his reads:
  - ❑ O5 deep
  - ❑ O2 cutting diagonally in front of him
  - ❑ O1 flashing into the middle
  - ❑ O3 for a reversal

Player O5:

- Starts on the offensive foul line and waits for the second pass to go opposite.

STEP SEVEN

Screen-and-Roll for O1 and O2

Under excellent face guard or denial pressure, and none of the options appear open, then this step is activated. This step permits the up-man (O2) to go screen-and-roll for the half-court player on the side of the ball. (See Figure 3-7.)

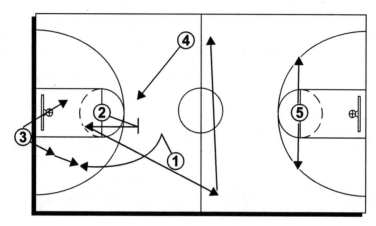

Figure 3-7

Player O1:

- Receives a screen from O2 and comes to meet the ball.

- If O1 catches the ball, he makes his reads:

  ❑ O5 deep

  ❑ O2 crossing diagonally in front of the ball toward the sidelines

  ❑ O4 flashing to the middle

  ❑ O3 as the reverse man

- If O2 catches the inbounds pass, then O1 gets back to the initial position on the ballside and prepares to cross the floor.

Player O2:

- Turns and sets a screen for O1 and as soon as O1 clears his line of vision, rolls back to the inbounder coming to meet the ball.

- If O2 receives the pass, he makes his reads:

  ❑ O5 deep

  ❑ O1 on his side

- ❏ O4 flashing to the middle

- ❏ O3 as the reverse man

- If O1 catches the first pass, O2 cuts diagonally in front of him, wide to the sideline.

- If not open on the sideline, he quickly crosses the floor, back to the far sideline.

Player O3:

- Inbounds the ball to either O1 or O2 and then steps in behind that player.

- Looks for the reversal so he can swing it to the wide sideline.

Player O4:

- Waits to see which player receives the inbounds pass and then makes his diagonal cut to the middle of the floor, getting good spacing depending on where the ball was caught.

- If he receives the ball, his reads are the same as previously described.

Player O5:

- Starts on the offensive foul line and reacts opposite to the second pass.

STEP EIGHT

Screen-and-Roll for O2 and O4

This step is the same as the seventh, except that this time the up-man goes to screen-and-roll for the half-court player opposite the ball. (See Figure 3-8.)

Player O1:

- Waits to see who receives the inbounds pass and then makes the diagonal cut to the middle of the floor, getting good spacing depending on where the ball was caught.

- Always comes to meet the ball, never letting the ball come to him.

- If he receives the ball, his reads are:

- ❏ first to O5 deep

- ❏ second to dribble the ball upcourt

- ❏ third to O2 or O4 wide on the opposite sideline

- ❏ fourth to O3 in a trailing position for the reversal

Player O2:

- Turns and sets a screen for O4.

- As soon as O4 has cleared his line of vision, O2 rolls back to the ball, making sure to meet it in the air.

- If O2 catches the ball, he makes his reads:

  ❑ O5 deep

  ❑ O4 on the same-side sideline

  ❑ O1 flashing diagonally into the middle of the floor

  ❑ O3 for a reversal

- If O4 catches the ball on the inbounds pass, he cuts diagonally in front of O4 looking for a pass as he heads to the ballside sideline.

- If not open on that cut, quickly crosses to the other side of the floor and remains wide on the sideline with his back toward the sideline.

Player O3:

- Inbounds the ball to either O4 coming off the screen set by O2, or O2 rolling back to the ball.

- Steps in and gets good spacing behind whichever player he inbounded the ball to.

- Looks to receive a reverse pass and swing it wide to the sideline area.

Player O4:

- Sets himself up to receive a screen from O2 and then cuts hard as he comes to meet the ball.

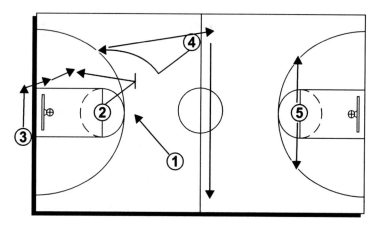

Figure 3-8

- If O4 receives the inbound pass, he makes his reads:
  - ❑ O5 deep
  - ❑ O2 crossing diagonally in front of the ball toward the near sideline
  - ❑ O1 flashing into the middle
  - ❑ O3 trailing the play for a reversal
- If O2 catches the inbounds pass, he gets in line on the ballside sideline looking for a pass up court from O2.
- If he is not open in that position, he quickly follows his rule and crosses the floor to get wide on the opposite sideline with his back toward the sideline.

Player O5:

- Gets to his initial starting position on the foul line on the offensive end of the floor.
- Waits to read the second pass and then reacts by going to the opposite side of the court from that pass.

Summary

You now have all eight steps in building your press breaker. This is a complete offense in itself and will break any press you face.

However, later chapters will explain how to bring up two players, then three players, and then four to give you the same offense with a change of pace. You can actually confuse your opponents by merely changing the number of players you bring up to frontcourt.

CHAPTER 4

Breakdown Drills for the 1-Up Press Breaker

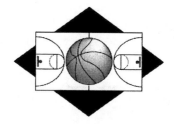

Most coaches use the *whole-part-whole* method to teach their players offensive and defensive techniques and tactics. This chapter presents the part (drills) system, describing the drills for each part of the 1-up press breaker, and is divided into the first pass series and the second pass series.

By using fewer players in a more structured drill, the players get more repetition and learn the techniques and tactics more quickly. Also, players often have more intensity and deeper concentration when drilling because they know the coach can more easily recognize when they are making mistakes.

THE FIRST PASS SERIES

Inbounding the Ball Versus Denial Pressure

Procedure:

• Line up players as shown in Figure 4-1. Make sure all candidates for the O2 position drill on getting free from denial pressure.

- O3 can run the baseline. If O3 inbounds the pass to O2, O3 moves to his proper trailing position.

- O2 tries to free himself by using a change of pace, a change of direction, V-cuts, stutter steps, stops-and-goes, or any other maneuver he wishes to try.

- X2 tries to prevent O2 from receiving the inbounds pass.

- X3 tries to alter O3's vision by keeping his hands up and moving in the same plane as O3 holds the basketball, hoping to force a lob pass or a bounce pass — both slower passes and more easily intercepted or deflected.

- If X2 or X3 intercepts a pass, he fast breaks against O2 and O3.

- If O2 receives the pass, O2 squares up while O3 gets to his trailing position.

- If the ball is successfully inbounded, O2 and O3 try to advance the ball to the other end of the court against X2 and X3.

- Run the drill as many times as you wish. You should run the drill after any game in which you had trouble inbounding the ball.

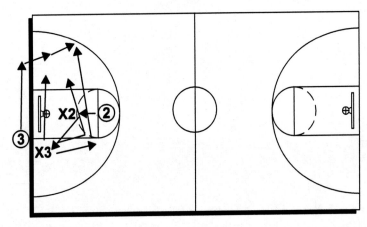

Figure 4-1

Objectives:

- To teach O3 and O2 to communicate and get the pass inbounded.

- To teach O3 to fake pass, run the baseline to get the proper angle, make the pass at the exact moment for completion, and move to his proper trailing position if he successfully passes the ball inbounds.

- To teach O2 to use maneuvers to get himself open for the pass.

- To teach X2 to play proper denial defense.

- To teach X3 to get his arms in the plane of the ball so that O3 will have to make a slower pass that's easier to intercept.
- To teach the first part of the 1-up press breaker.
- To condition.

Inbounding the Ball Versus 2-Man Pressure

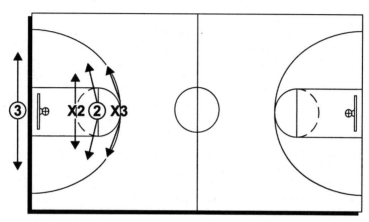

Figure 4-2

Procedure:

- Line up players as shown in Figure 4-2. X2 and X3 can play on each side of O2. X2 and X3 can play with X2 face guarding and X3 playing behind O2. Or, X2 can play denial while X3 plays center field, trying to prevent the lob pass.
- O3 can run the baseline. If O3 successfully completes the pass, he steps in at the proper trailing position.
- O2 uses his maneuvers to try to free himself for an inbounds pass.
- O3 must have a clock in his head, knowing when five seconds is about to expire, judiciously calling a time-out.
- If X2 and X3 intercept the pass, they fast break against O2 and O3.
- If the ball is successfully inbounded, O2 and O3 fast break to their offensive end of the court against X2 and X3.

Objectives:

- To teach O2 to use maneuvers to free himself from double-teaming denial defense.
- To teach O3 the proper moment and the correct angle to enter the pass.

- To teach O3 to step in at the proper trailing position.
- To teach O2 and O3 to defend if the pass is intercepted.
- To teach O2 and O3 to blow the ball up the floor if they gain an advantage.
- To teach the first part of the 1-up press breaker.
- To condition.

Inbounding to O1 or O4

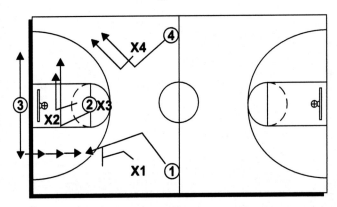

Figure 4-3

Procedure:

- Line up players as shown in Figure 4-3. X3 is shown playing center field, but X3 could play on O3, or X3 could double-team O2. You could let X3 decide and let him change from possession to possession, or you could require X3 to use the tactic of your next opponent.
- O2 must try to free himself. If he's able to do so, O3 passes to O2.
- If O1 sees O2 cannot free himself, O1 tries to free himself from X1's denial pressure. O1 breaks toward O3 and the ball.
- If O4 sees O3 running the baseline, and if O4 sees O2 unable to free himself for the inbounds pass, then O4 tries to free himself from X4's denial pressure. O4 breaks toward O3 and the ball.
- If the defense intercepts a pass, they fast break.
- If the offense gets the ball inbounds, the player receiving the pass squares up. O3 should move to his proper trailing position when the ball is successfully inbounded.
- This drill leads directly into the one explained next in Figure 4-4.

Objectives:

- To teach O1, O2, O3, and O4 their responsibilities for getting the ball inbounded.

- To teach O1, O2, O3, and O4 to identify the defense they're facing and prepare to get the ball in.

- To teach X1, X2, X3, and X4 to play proper denial defense.

- To teach the first part of the 1-up press breaker.

Making Cuts off of the First Pass

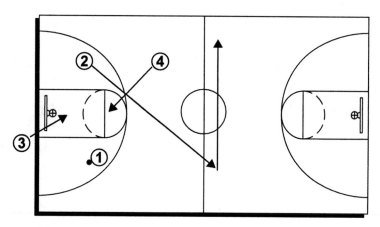

Figure 4-4

Procedure:

- This continuation of Figure 4-3 is only one of the three places O3 could have inbounded the ball. The defenders have been eliminated from the diagram (See Figure 4-4) to prevent clutter; but X1 would cover O1, X2 would cover O2, etc.

- In Figure 4-3, the ball was inbounded to O1, so you do the same here. Figure 4-4 illustrates the proper cutting maneuvers by O2, O3, and O4. O2 makes the diagonal cut, checks for O1's move, and then crosses to the other sideline. O4 flash pivots. O3 steps in at the proper trailing position.

- If the ball had been passed into O2, it would have activated the cuts shown in Figure 3-1. If the ball had been passed into O4, the players would have run the cuts in Figure 3-6.

- You can require the defenders to play man-to-man defense after the ball is inbounded. Or, you can require the defenders to run a trap and an umbrella, simulating a zone press. If running the trap and umbrella, X1 and X3 would have trapped O1 while X2 and X4 would have moved to the interception positions of the umbrella.

- If the defense intercepts, they fast break.
- If the offense breaks the press, they fast break.

Objectives:

- To teach O3 to make the proper inbounds pass.
- To teach O1, O2, and O4 to use maneuvers to free themselves for the proper inbounds pass.
- To teach O1, O2, O3, and O4 the proper cuts to make when the ball has been inbounded.
- To teach X1, X2, X3, and X4 how to play denial defense and how to form a trap and an umbrella, whether running a zone or a man-to-man press.
- To teach O1, O2, O3, and O4 to get organized to stop a fast break if any pass is intercepted.
- To teach O1, O2, O3, and O4 how to fast break should they break the press.
- To teach poise and control under pressure.
- To condition.

O2 and O1 Using the Screen-and-Roll

Procedure:

- Line up players as shown in Figure 4-5, which illustrates the pass being inbounded to O1; O2, O3, and O4 read this pass and make their proper cuts. Again, the defenders have been eliminated to prevent clutter.
- In this figure, X3 double-teams with X2 on O2. X3 can stay with this double-team when O2 goes to set the screen for O1, or X3 can help X1 cover O1.
- Use only X1, X2, and X3, playing X3 on O1, on O3, or on O2.
- O4 is only shown in Figure 4-5 so O4 can make his proper cuts when the ball is inbounded to either O2 or O1. (Figure 4-6 brings into play O4 and X4.)
- Once the ball is inbounded, the players cut as shown in Figure 3-7.
- Defenders can play the screen-and-roll with a switch, a double-team on the screener, a double-team on the roller, or let each defender guard his own assignment. It's best to use the defense of your next opponent.

- If the defense intercepts a pass, they fast break.

- Once O1 or O2 receives the inbounds pass, they square up and the attackers away from the ball make their proper cuts. This ends the offensive part of the drill.

Objectives:

- To teach O1, O2, and O3 to cooperate in the screen-and-roll to get the ball inbounds against teams that employ great pressure.

- To teach O1, O2, O3, and O4 to make the proper cuts when the ball is inbounded.

- To teach the defense to use proper defensive techniques to prevent the ball from being inbounded. When activating the entire defense, to run either the man-to-man press, or the trap and umbrella. The offense would fast break when they break the press.

- To teach the offense to switch quickly to defense in case of an interception.

- To teach poise and control when facing teams with great defensive pressure.

- To condition.

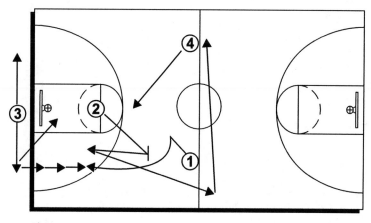

Figure 4-5

O2 and O4 Using the Screen-and-Roll

Procedures:

- Line up players as shown in Figure 4-6. The defenders have been eliminated to prevent clutter.

- X3 and X2 doubled-teamed O2, so O2 cannot get the inbounds pass.

- When O4 saw O3 running the baseline and O2 coming to set the screen, O4 began to set up X4 (not shown) for O2's screen.

- O4 is the open receiver.

- O2 runs his route for a possible pass from O4. When O2 sees O1 flashing to the middle for a possible pass from O4, O2 cuts to the weakside sideline.

- O3 steps in to his trailing position.

- Defenders can play the screen-and-roll with a switch, with a double-team of one of the receivers, with a center fielder, etc. Defenders should mix their coverages or play the defense of your next opponent.

- If the defense intercepts a pass, they fast break.

Objectives:

- To teach O2, O3, and O4 to cooperate in the screen-and-roll to get the ball inbounds against teams that employ great pressure.

- To teach O1, O2, O3, and O4 to make the proper cuts when the ball is inbounded.

- To teach the defense to use proper defensive techniques to prevent the ball from being inbounded. (When activating the entire defense, run either the man-to-man press or the trap and umbrella. The offense would fast break when they break the press.)

- To teach the offense to switch quickly to defense in case of an interception.

- To teach poise and control when facing teams with great defensive pressure.

- To condition.

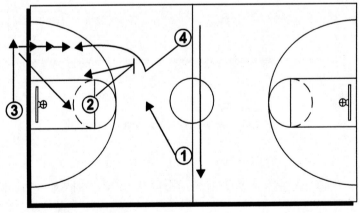

Figure 4-6

THE SECOND PASS SERIES

Pass from O2 to O1

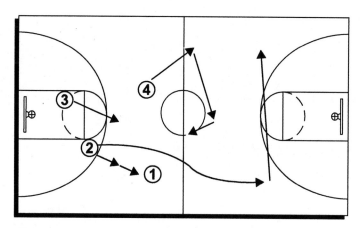

Figure 4-7

Procedure:

- Line up players as shown in Figure 4-7. The defenders have been eliminated to prevent clutter.

- If the defenders play their assignments man-to-man, O2 dribbles as far as he can up the floor. Any time O1 gets open, O2 passes to O1 who advances the ball by dribbling.

- If covered by a trap and umbrella, X3 and X2 trap O2 by simulating a zone press.

- Or, you could have defense play straight box-1 zone until O2 passes the ball to O1, then have X2 and X1 trap O1, and X3 and X4 form the umbrella. This simulates a dropback zone press. When facing a dropback zone press or the box-1, O1 and O4 would not want to cross the half-court line, which is the major trapping area of dropback-zone presses and the 2-2-1 zone press.

- O1 could dribble, pass to O2, or pass to O4.

- If the defense intercepts, they fast break while the offense tries to stop them.

- If the offense breaks the press, they fast break.

- If running a zone press, you can really overload the situation by using six defenders. Have X1, X2, X3, and X4 defend their assignments, while X5 plays deep safety and X6 traps the ball no matter where it is. This really compels the offense to concentrate and intensify.

Objectives:

- To teach the cuts after the second pass, this time from O2 to O1.

- To teach the defense to play both man-to-man and zone presses.

- To teach the defenders how to form a trap and an umbrella.

- To teach the offense poise and control while attacking any press.

- To teach the offense to stop the opponent's fast break when a turnover occurs.

- To teach the fast-break attack after beating the press.

- To teach all the options of the 1-up press breaker.

- To teach proper decision-making by the offense.

Pass from O2 to O4

Procedure:

- Line up players as shown in Figure 4-8. The defenders have been eliminated to prevent clutter.

- If defenders play their assignments man-to-man, O2 dribbles as far as he can up the floor. Any time O1 can get open, O2 passes to O1 who advances the ball by dribbling. When O4 sees O1 cannot get open, O4 flashes to the middle and O2 begins to look for the pass there.

- If covered by a trap and umbrella, X3 and X2 trap O2 by simulating a zone press.

- Or, you could have defense play straight box-1 zone until O2 passes the ball to O4, then have X3 and X4 trap O1, and X1 and X2 form the umbrella. This simulates a dropback zone press. When facing a dropback-zone press or the box-1, O1 and O4 would not want to cross the half-court line, which is the major trapping area of dropback-zone presses and the 2-2-1 zone press.

- O4 can dribble, pass to O2 breaking up the sideline, or pass to O1 on his cut to the spot O4 just vacated.

- O3 finds his new trailing position.

- If the defense intercepts, they fast break while the offense tries to stop the fast break.

- If the offense breaks the press, they fast break.

- If running a zone press, you can really overload the situation by using six defenders. Have X1, X2, X3, and X4 defend their assignments, while X5 plays deep safety and X6 traps the ball no matter where it is. This really compels the offense to concentrate and intensify.

Objectives:

- To teach the cuts after the second pass, this time from O2 to O4.
- To teach the defense to play both man-to-man and zone presses.
- To teach the defenders how to form a trap and an umbrella.
- To teach the offense poise and control while attacking any press.
- To teach the offense to stop the opponent's fast break when a turnover occurs.
- To teach the fast-break attack after beating the press.
- To teach all the options of the 1-up press breaker.
- To teach proper decision-making by the offense.

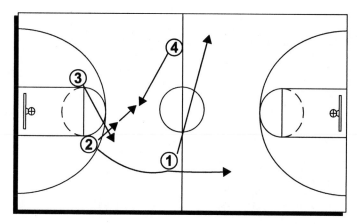

Figure 4-8

Reversal Pass to O3

Procedures:

- Line up players as shown in Figure 4-9. The defenders have been eliminated to prevent clutter.
- When no options are open, O2 reverses the ball to O3 and the attack begins again.
- O3 can advance the ball by dribbling until the defense stops him.
- O1 flashes to the middle, and if he's not open, O1 replaces O2 as a possible throw-back receiver.

- When O2 makes the reversal pass to O3, O2 cuts up the middle for a possible return pass. O2 continues up to the strongside sideline and reads the next pass.

- O4 moves out of the middle lane when he sees O2 cannot make the pass to him. When O4 sees the reversal pass to O3, O4 moves to the weakside sideline.

- From these positions, the offense begins again based on where the next pass goes.

- If the defense intercepts any pass, they fast break and the original offense tries

- If the offense breaks the press, they fast break.

Objectives:

- To teach the cuts after the second pass, this time from O2 to O3.
- To teach the defense to play both man-to-man and zone presses.
- To teach the defenders how to form a trap and an umbrella.
- To teach the offense poise and control while attacking any press.
- To teach the offense to stop the opponent's fast break when a turnover occurs.
- To teach the fast-break attack after beating the press.
- To teach all the options of the 1-up press breaker.
- To teach proper decision-making by the offense.

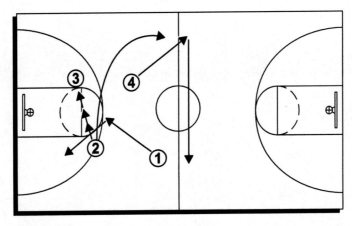

Figure 4-9

Pass To The Post

Procedure:

- Line up players as shown in Figure 4-10, which shows the players making their cuts as the ball is inbounded to O2, then O2 making the long pass to O5. This pass can be made from the inbound passer (O3), or as a second pass once the ball is inbounded. Figure 4-10 illustrates it as a second pass (from O3 to O2 to O5), but it could be from O3 to O5, from O1 to O5, or from O4 to O5. This is always the first option on the press breaker.

- You can only use a defender on the pass thrower and the post man (O5), or you can use the full defense described in the previous drills, including six defenders.

- When drilling on O5 receiving the pass, you could allow only one defender, X5.

Objectives:

- To teach the long pass, the first option of the press breaker.
- To teach the offense their cuts, even if the pass is made to the deep attacker.

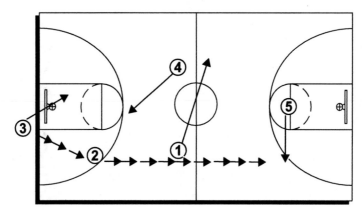

Figure 4-10

Summary

You now have all eight steps of the 1-up press breaker and corresponding breakdown drills. You can use these breakdown drills in two ways: first, apply them to teach the cuts of the press breaker from the first or second pass, and second, to drill individuals on their fundamentals.

During your season you can use the first five chapters as your complete press breaker. It's really all you need. Later chapters will present the 2-up, 3-up, and 4-up press breakers so you can thoroughly confuse even the best pressing teams.

CHAPTER 5

1-Up Press Breaker Versus the Basic Presses

Most of you will face the 2-2-1 zone press, the 1-2-1-1 zone press, and a man-to-man press that traps and umbrellas. A few teams will match your original formation and then go to a trap and an umbrella when the ball is inbounded. How you attack those presses off the first and second passes is presented in detail in this chapter.

1-UP PRESS BREAKER VERSUS THE 2-2-1

Figure 5-1 illustrates the inbounds pass to O2. The other four players make their cuts based on this inbounds pass. Because of the unique nature of the cuts in the press breaker, a 2-2-1 zone press should offer no trouble. The opponent would have to make adjustments to stop your first pass from being successful.

Let's explore the options available from the simple inbounds pass to O2. O3 steps in to his trailing position. O1 saw the pass come into O2, so O1 cuts to the opposite sideline and faces inbounds. O4 flash pivots for a possible pass from O2.

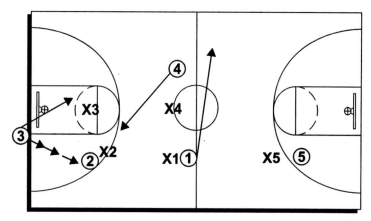

Figure 5-1

The previous cuts leave X1 guarding space; there's no attacker there. O1 has moved to the spot vacated by O4. This puts too much pressure on X4 who cannot cover both the flash-pivot cut of O4 and the overhead pass to O1. X5 is busy guarding the post player deep.

If X4 decides to stay deep on O1, then X3 must decide to cover either O3 or O4. If X3 drops to cover O4, then the reverse pass to O3 leaves either a quick pass to O4 or a quick pass to O1 as the second pass. If X3 is slow to cover O4 or decides to cover O3, then a pass to O4 leaves X4 having to cover either O1 or the dribbling O4.

By O3 taking the proper trailing position, X3 cannot possibly cover the middle passing lane and the pass back to O3. And by O4 flashing into the middle lane until X4 can no longer front him, it makes X4's coverage impossible. When X4 has to leave the fronting position, it leaves O4 open for the flash-pivot pass. But if X4 stays with O4 in a fronting position, then no one is available to cover O1. Either way, the press is broken.

Your first pass against the basic 2-2-1 zone press is a press breaker. Unless the defense makes an adjustment, or your players make the wrong decision, you now have the fast break, and your opponents will be coming out of their press in a hurry.

But just for the sake of discussion, let's say your players did not see the openings (and that's what the drills in Chapter 4 are all about), so you have to make a second pass. Any second pass in the 1-up press breaker series will also break the 2-2-1 zone press.

Figure 5-2 illustrates the 2-2-1 zone press coverage with a pass to the flash-pivot cutter (O4). O4 can immediately throw an overhead-flip pass to the deep O5 if X5 does not have him covered. But if X5 has O5 covered, then no defender is available to cover O1, who cut to the weakside sideline. So O4 pivots and passes to O1, who begins a three-lane break using the dribble.

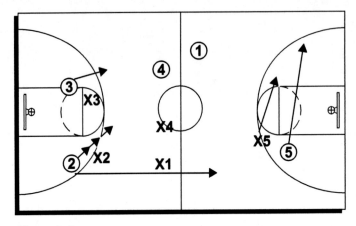

Figure 5-2

But what if X1 chased O1? Then who has O2 cutting up the original strongside sideline? A pass from O4 to O2 gets the three-lane fast break going with O2 handling the ball.

If X4 drifted back to cover O2, then O4 has the dribble down the middle of the court and the press is broken. If all else fails — and it won't fail if the players are making good decisions — O4 can pass back to the trailing O3.

O3 can make things much more difficult for X3 to cover both O3 and O4 by merely trailing at the proper angle. He should spread away from and be slightly behind X3. O4 performs the same maneuver on X4. By flashing a little farther toward O2, it becomes an impossible coverage assignment for X4. He cannot deny the pass to O4 and still cover the overhead-flip pass to O1.

1-UP PRESS BREAKER VERSUS THE 1-2-1-1

Figure 5-3 illustrates a first pass attack against the diamond-and-one press (1-2-1-1), and Figure 5-4 illustrates a second pass attack against the same defense. Usually all you need to break the zone press are the first-pass steps; but sometimes players will not spot the open attacker, and then you need the second-pass attack.

O3 passes to O2 and steps in to take his trailing position (Figure 5-3). When O4 sees the pass being inbounded to O2, O4 flash pivots. O1 takes a step or two toward O2 before cutting to the opposite-side sideline.

When the ball is inbounded to O2, X3 and X2 are trained in the diamond-and-one press to trap the first pass. X1 and X4 provide the umbrella coverage, and X5 covers deep safety.

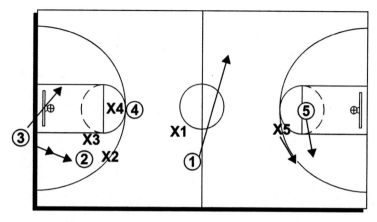

Figure 5-3

At the beginning of the first pass attack, O2 has three outlets: to O3 trailing, to O4 posting, and to O1 up the sideline. But O1 leaves when he sees he is covered by X1. This leaves X1 guarding space, and forces X4 to cover three receivers: X4 can cover the flashing O4 or the trailing O3, or X4 can split them, watching O2 for a cue of the direction O2 intends to pass. But X4 won't be able to cover the overhead-flip pass to O1 on the far sideline. X5 is covering O5, preventing O2 from throwing the ball deep.

The pass to O1 should easily produce the three-lane fast-break attack against the press with O1, your best ball handler, dribbling as the lead guard. A pass to O4 would also see O4 pivoting, then passing to O1.

Sometimes your players don't see these openings, or a player will make the pass too quickly before an opening occurs. When that happens, your second pass series begins.

Figure 5-4 illustrates a second pass attack. The ball has been inbounded to O2 (not shown in the figure). O2 then spots O1 coming to meet the ball, and O2 quickly passes to O1.

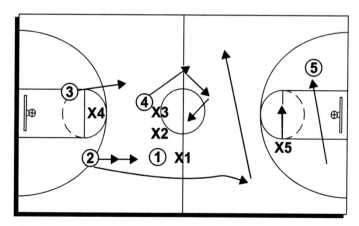

Figure 5-4

After O2 passes to O1, O2 cuts around O1 up the sideline. If O2 does not get the pass back from O1, O2 cuts to the opposite-side sideline. O4 moves on up the floor before coming back at the proper angle to flash pivot. O3 cuts up the floor creating a new trailing position. O5, on the second pass, is taught to go opposite.

X1 and X2 now must trap O1 per the 1-2-1-1 press rules. X3 and X4 provide the umbrella. X5 is still safety.

O1 is your best ball handler. He can use the step-through maneuver, take a retreat dribble before driving around one of the defenders, or begin his passing checks. His checks in the correct order are: O5 deep, O2 cutting up the near sideline, O4 flash pivoting, O3 in the trailing position for reversal of the ball. Any pass to O2, O4, or O5 breaks the press, and the fast break results.

O1 can read X4 and X3. X4, when O2 cuts to the far sideline, is left guarding space. X3 must cover 3, 4, and O2. X3 cannot do that, so the press should be easily broken.

1-UP PRESS BREAKER VERSUS MAN-TO-MAN

You can play the man-to-man press a million and one different ways. Defenders can allow you to get the ball in, then go trap. They can let you get the ball in but not go trap until you take the first dribble. They can deny you the ball and when you get the ball in, they go trap. They can face guard and trap only after you have taken the first dribble. These are only three of a myriad of tactics.

But it doesn't matter which you face. Just have the players stay poised and execute the offense. You have all that's needed to break any man-to-man press that matches up man for man and then creates a trap and an umbrella.

Figure 5-5 shows O1 with the basketball. How did O1 get the ball inbounded to him? He and O2 ran the screen-and-roll pattern shown in Figure 3-7. The defense has stayed man-to-man, intending to trap when O1 begins his dribble. Remember, O1 is your point guard, your best ball handler, and this is the way the opponents intend to disrupt your offense.

O1 begins his dribble. X1 cuts him off as in the zigzag drill presented in Chapter 1. X3 leaves the trailing O3 to double-team O1 with X1. O1 should keep his dribble alive, trying to retreat dribble, etc., until he can drive by the trap on either side.

Upon seeing the trap, X2 and X4 race to set the umbrella. X5 stays at safety. If X2 and X4 stay with their assignments, then a pass to O3 with O3 driving hard to midcourt, breaks the press. So X2 and X4 get in the passing lanes, covering three attackers. This leaves O1 with a pass crosscourt to O2 on the opposite sideline, and the press is broken.

If X4 drops to cover that pass, then O4 is open. O4 pivots, does his reads, and maybe even dribbles the ball into frontcourt.

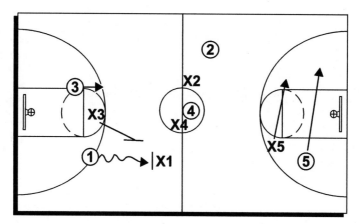

Figure 5-5

Summary

There are too many defensive variations of zone presses and man-to-man traps to ever be covered in a book. However, the three examples given here should show you how the 1-up press breaker defeats any defensive maneuver.

But you might want to have options or make adjustments, especially against teams that almost prevent you from inbounding the ball, so the 2-up press breaker is presented in Chapter 6.

CHAPTER 6

2-Up Press Breaker

The techniques and strategies of the 2-up press breaker aren't difficult to learn once you've learned the 1-up — same cuts, same decision making, same sequence of reads.

The difference is that you bring O1 up to the area around the top of the key. O2 drops to somewhere near the low-blocks to screen for O1. You can allow a fake screen or permit O2 to go toward O1 and have O1 make individual cuts. O4 moves over to take the original spot of O1, and O5 leaves the deep spot to take the place O4's just vacated spot.

Why would you need this addition to your press breaker? One day you will face a tremendous defensive duo who can almost single-handedly keep you from getting the ball inbounds. When that occurs, you'll need the 2-up press breaker.

You can also use the 2-up press breaker as a change-up to confuse good defensive pressure ball clubs. Altering your set slightly can compel the defenders to alter their strategy somewhat.

There are three primary options for the 2-up press breaker: screen-and-roll with O2 receiving the inbounds pass, screen-and-roll with O1 receiving the inbounds pass, and O4 or O5 receiving the first pass.

For secondary options, let O2 fake setting the screen-and-roll, or permit both O1 and O2 to merely cut to get open. Regardless of whether O1 or O2 gets open to receive the inbounds pass, the attack is the same as in the primary options. This just gives you two more ways to confuse exceptionally good face guard defenders. All these tactics receive individual attention in this chapter.

SCREEN-AND-ROLL WITH O2 RECEIVING THE INBOUNDS PASS

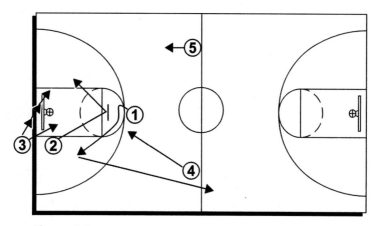

Figure 6-1

Player O1:

- Begins at the top of the key, sets up his man, and cuts off O2's screen either way. (See Figure 6-1.)

- When O2 receives the inbounds pass, he fills sideline wide.

Player O2:

- Starts on the ballside block and screens up for O1.

- Reads which direction O1 uses his screens and then opens and rolls opposite.

- When he catches the ball, he makes his reads in order:

  ❑ O5 on the near sideline

  ❑ O4 flashing to the ball

  ❑ O1 on the opposite sideline wide

  ❑ O3 in proper trailing position for the reversal

Player O3:

- Inbounds the ball to either O1 coming off the screen or O2 rolling back to the ball. He reads whether or not the defenders switch. If X2 switches to O1, then O2 is the primary receiver. If X1 tries to fight over the screen, then O1 is the primary receiver.

- Stays behind the ball at the correct angle and spacing as the reverse man.

Player O4:

- If O2 catches the ball on the side opposite him, he flashes to the middle of the court.

- Remains in the middle of the floor keeping good spacing as the ball is advanced. He may fake leaving, then flash back to the ball.

Player O5:

- If O2 catches the ball on the side of the floor where O5 is located, he remains on that side of the floor looking for a pass down that sideline.

- Remains on the same sideline and maintains proper spacing as the ball is advanced.

SCREEN-AND-ROLL WITH O1 RECEIVING THE INBOUNDS PASS

Player O1:

- Begins at the top of the key, waits for O2's screen, and uses it to cut either right or left toward the ball. (See Figure 6-2.)

- If he catches the ball, he reads beginning on the same side of the court and then goes across the floor to the opposite side in this order:

  - ❏ O4 on his same-side sideline

  - ❏ O5 flashing diagonally to the middle of the floor

  - ❏ O2 who has filled the lane on the sideline vacated by O5

  - ❏ O3 on a reversal

Player O2:

- Starts on the ballside block and screens for O1.

- Waits for O1 to use the screen and then rolls opposite back to the ball.

- After O1 catches the ball, he fills the sideline vacated by O5 and stays sideline wide.

Player O3:

- Inbounds the ball and steps in as the reverse man and safety.

Player O4:

- Sees that the ball was inbounded to his side, so he stays on the same sideline looking for the second pass or keeps good spacing as the ball is advanced.

Player O5:

- Sees that the ball was inbounded opposite him, so he flashes in to the middle of the floor looking for the second pass or keeps good spacing as the ball is advanced.

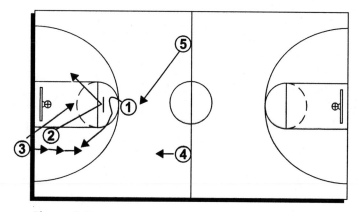

Figure 6-2

O4 OR O5 RECEIVING THE FIRST PASS

Player O1:

- As the ball is inbounded to O5, cuts diagonally in front of the ball to the same sideline. (See Figure 6-3.)

- Remains on that sideline looking for the second pass and keeps good spacing as the ball is advanced.

Player O2:

- Sees that O5 has received the inbounds pass and fills the sideline vacated by O4.

- Stays on that sideline looking for the second pass or keeps good spacing as the ball is advanced.

Player O3:

- Runs the baseline toward O5, which is the cue for O5 to V-cut to the ball.
- After inbounding the ball, steps in as the reverse man and safety.

Player O4:

- Reads the inbounds pass and flashes diagonally to the middle.
- Remains in the middle of the floor looking for the second pass or keeps good spacing as the ball advances.

Player O5:

- Reads O3 running the baseline and V-cuts toward the ball.
- As he catches and squares to get vision up the floor, he makes his reads:
  - ❏ O1 diagonally cutting the same sideline
  - ❏ O4 flashing to the middle
  - ❏ O2 on the opposite sideline wide
  - ❏ O3 on a reversal
- If the ball is inbounded to O4, O4 and O5 simply exchange responsibilities.

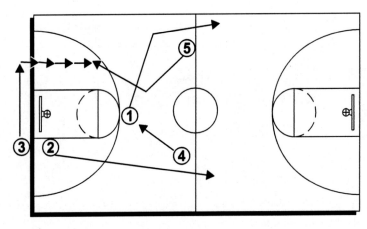

Figure 6-3

O1 AND O2 FAKE THE SCREEN-AND-ROLL

Figure 6-1 and 6-2 illustrate the screen-and-roll by O1 and O2. Instead of setting the screen-and-roll, O2 has been reading X2 switching. So O2 goes to set the screen, but instead pivots and breaks back toward the ball, just before O1 cuts off the screen and just before X2 makes his *switch* call. We call this maneuver *splitting the switch*.

This confuses the defenders. Both would probably go with O1 once, and the next time, both might even follow O2 before making the adjustment of not switching. When that happens, O2 goes back to setting the screen-and-roll, which always frees O1.

The cuts remain the same once the ball is inbounded.

You may use this tactic as a change of pace, or to force the defenders to readjust their thinking on switching or not switching.

O1 AND O2 JUST CUTTING TO GET OPEN

This is another adjustment to the screen-and-roll. When the coach feels the defense is adjusting to the screen-and-roll, or when the defense begins to successfully deny the inbounds pass, it's a good time to make an offensive adjustment. One adjustment that really works is to allow both O1 and O2 to use individual cuts to free themselves for the inbounds pass. O2 begins from the low-block strongside and may cut to either side instead of going to set the screen for O1. O1 can read this, so O1 uses his individual cuts to free himself to the other side of the court. The cuts after the ball has been inbounded remain the same.

You may use this strategy as a change of pace, or force the defenders to readjust their defensive tactics. This is especially useful when the defense begins to read your screen-and-roll and makes successful defensive adjustments against it.

Summary

You now have a change-up in strategy to further attack and confuse the defense. It looks like an entirely new offense, but you have little new to teach.

The 2-up press breaker is also a very good tactic to use when the defense begins to give O2 and O3 trouble while trying to get the ball inbounded successfully. By bringing another good ball handler down to help get the ball in, you force the defense to make another adjustment. Often that adjustment is more complicated for the defense than the offense because the offense still runs the same cuts; they just begin from a slightly different formation.

CHAPTER 7

Breakdown Drills for the 2-Up Press Breaker

You now have two different formations for starting your press breaker: the 1-up formation and the 2-up formation. You also have drills to help you teach the 1-up formation.

This chapter outlines four drills to teach the 2-up press breaker and these drills will give your players a feeling of confidence knowing they have more than adequate means of breaking any press. You'll have the 3-on-3 drill for O1, O2, and O3. You could include O4 and O5 without any defenders so that you can run your cuts once you get the ball inbounds. Then you'll have the split-the-screen drill for O1 and O2 and their defenders. And finally you'll have the individual-cuts drill for both O1 and O2 and their defenders.

3-ON-3 FOR O1, O2, AND O3

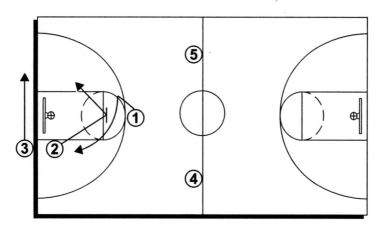

Figure 7-1

Procedure:

- Line up players as shown in Figure 7-1. You can use only O1, O2, and O3 and their defenders X1, X2, and X3 (not shown so as not to clutter the figure), but by adding O4 and O5, you'll be able to run the first- and second-pass series.

- O2 starts at the big block on the ballside. O1 starts at the top of the key. O3 is allowed to run the baseline.

- X1 and X2 face guard. X3 can begin on the ball or play shortstop (double with X1 on O1, or double with X2 on O2). Or X3 can play center field just above the key looking to help on any lob pass into either O1 or O2.

- You can mix the way X3 plays defense from possession to possession or use the defensive system of your next opponent.

- O2 goes to screen for O1. O1 sets up X1 for the screen by dipping in one direction before breaking opposite. This dip keys O2 where to set his screen. O2 should set his screen so that X1 would have to go under the screen to get back on O1. Just as X1 attempts to go under the screen, O2 should roll, O2 making sure his roll is back toward the ball but in the opposite direction of O1's cut.

- O3 reads X2's defense to determine who will be the primary receiver. If X2 switches, O2 is the primary receiver. If X2 tells X1 to stay with O1, then O1 becomes the primary receiver. O3 must move so that he will always be at the proper angle to pass the ball inbounds.

- If the defense intercepts the pass, they fast break, and O1, O2, and O3 must prevent the lay-up.

- If the ball is successfully inbounded, the receiver of the inbounds pass squares up while his teammates run their respective cuts. If you wish, make a second pass and run the cuts off the second series. The offense fast breaks to the opposite end of the court with X1, X2, and X3 defending.

Objectives:

- To teach proper screen-and-roll methods.
- To teach O3 to read the defense so he can locate the primary receiver.
- To teach the cuts of the first- and second-pass series.
- To teach face guard and denial defense.
- To teach shortstopping, center fielding, and pressure on the passer.
- To teach stopping the opponent's fast break off interceptions.
- To teach fast breaking off your press breaker.
- To condition.

SPLIT-THE-SCREEN

Procedure:

- Line up players as shown in Figure 7-2. Defenders have been omitted, but X1 covers O1, X2 blankets O2, and X3 defends O3. You will need to add O4 and O5 if you intend to run the cuts off the first and second pass.
- O2 goes to set the screen for O1. O1 dips to set up the screen opposite where he intends to cut. But just as O2 gets to the proper spot to set the screen, he peels off toward same side O1 dipped. This usually leaves X2 and X1 both guarding O1 if they intended to *switch*. And it will leave them both guarding O2 if they did not intend to switch. This is a great maneuver to use against a team that switches. It confuses the defenders. And just when they go to not switching, you change your strategy and allow O2 to set the screen for O1.
- X3 can play on the passer (O3). Or X3 can play shortstop, center field, or mix it up.
- If you add O4 and O5 (not shown), you can run your first-pass cuts.
- If the defense steals the ball, they fast break against O1, O2, and O3.
- If the offense successfully enters the ball and makes the second pass (if you are using that), they fast break against X1, X2, and X3.

Objectives:

- To teach getting the ball inbounds against *switching* defenses.

- To teach proper mechanics of splitting-the-screen.

- To teach the cuts off the first-pass and second-pass series.

- To teach shortstopping, center fielding, and pressure on the passer.

- To teach stopping the opponent's fast break off interceptions.

- To teach fast breaking using the 2-up press breaker.

- To condition.

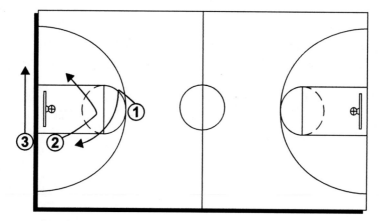

Figure 7-2

INDIVIDUAL CUTS FOR O1 AND O2

This drill gives more freedom of choice to O1 and O2; however, more control can be exercised by teaching only a few individual moves and giving O1 and O2 a few rules about movement. This change in strategy is more than worth the effort to teach because it will thoroughly confuse the defenders.

Procedure:

- Line up players as shown in Figure 7-3. O4 and O5 have been left out and so have the defenders. But if you intend to run the cuts off the first and second pass series, you'll need to use O4 and O5. X1 guards O1, X2 covers O2, etc.

- O1 and O2 can use whichever individual cuts you prefer to teach: the V-cut, step away then flash to the ball, change of pace, change of direction, seal maneuvers, etc.

- Both O1 and O2 can cut in the same direction, begin in the same direction and then cut opposite, etc.
- X3 can play on O3, play shortstop, or play center field.
- Once the ball is inbounded, the other players can run their first-pass cuts. Or you can drill the second-pass cuts if you prefer.
- If the offense successfully gets the press breaker going, they can fast break to the other end of the court.
- If the defenders intercept the pass, they fast break against O1, O2, and O3.

Objectives:

- To teach individual cutting maneuvers.
- To teach another change of strategy against your attackers.
- To teach the cuts off the first- and second-pass series.
- To teach fast breaking once your press breaker is successful.
- To teach shortstopping, center fielding, and pressure on the passer.
- To teach stopping the opponent's fast break off interceptions.
- To condition.

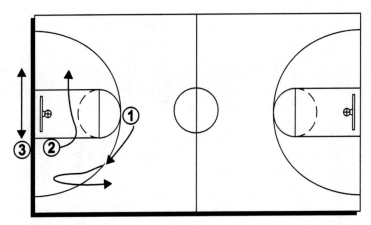

Figure 7-3

FRONTCOURT INDIVIDUAL CUTS

Procedure:

- Line up players as shown in Figure 7-4. No defenders are shown, but X3 guards O3, X4 is on O4, and X5 has O5.

- O4 and O5 use their individual cuts and reads of O3 to get open for a pass inbounds should O1 or O2 be unable to receive the inbounds pass.

- If the defense intercepts a pass, they fast break against O3, O4, and O5.

- If the pass is successfully inbounded, you can add O1 and O2 and run your first and second pass series.

- X4 can face guard O4, and X5 can face guard O5. When this occurs, you should let X3 play left field (a deeper position just over the half-court line). X3 can play on the passer, shortstop either O4 or O5, play center field and help as the cutters break toward the ball, or play left field looking to intercept the lob half-court pass. You should mix up this coverage or play the defense of your next opponent.

Objectives:

- To teach O4 and O5 some individual cuts to get open.

- To teach the first- and second-pass series (by adding O1 and O2).

- To teach defense on the passer, shortstopping, center fielding, and left fielding.

- To teach defense to fast break off of an interception, and to teach the offense how to quickly transfer to defense and stop the fast break.

- To teach the offense to fast break once they have beaten the press.

- To condition.

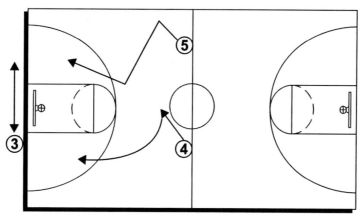

Figure 7-4

Summary

Your press breaker has now added several more options of getting the ball in against tremendous defensive pressure. It also gives your team several changes of strategy to confuse even the best pressure defenses.

The drills are designed not only to teach the cuts off the first and second pass of the offense, but to also teach maneuvers to get open. They use few players, which makes them much more competitive than a 5-on-5 scrimmage, requiring intensity and concentration from your squad. And the more you drill, the more muscle memory your players develop.

CHAPTER 8

3-Up Press Breaker

You already have two distinct formations from which to run the same press breaker. The 1-up press breaker doesn't offer the security of the 2-up press breaker as far as getting the ball inbounds is concerned, but both have the same cuts off the first and second passes.

Now we're adding a third formation, a 3-up press breaker, meaning we're bringing a third attacker up the floor. This way you can make a change in assignment to get your better ball handlers on the floor. Specifically, you can require O4 to throw the ball inbounds, designating O1, O2, and O3 as inbound receivers. Or you can still require O3 to throw the ball inbounds, and let O4 become the third inbounds receiver. After the ball is inbounded, you go back to your first- or second-pass series. Or you can follow the new cuts that are described later. Again, there are a myriad of options.

This chapter presents O4 throwing the ball inbounds with four options: inbounds pass to the middle-man (O3), inbounds pass to O1, inbounds pass to O2, and the reversal pass to O4 who steps inbounds at the trailing position.

INBOUNDS PASS TO THE MIDDLE-MAN

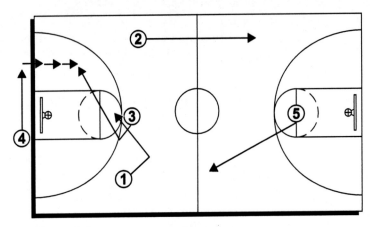

Figure 8-1

Player O1:

- As the ball is inbounded to O3 away from him, he flashes into the middle of the court. (See Figure 8-1.)
- Stays in the middle and keeps proper spacing as the ball is advanced.

Player O2:

- Sees that the ball is inbounded to O3 on his side of the floor, so he keeps proper spacing on the same-side sideline.

Player O3:

- Attempts to put a player who has good size in this position on the 3-up press breaker.
- Sets up his man and gets open going either direction.
- As he catches the ball and squares up, he makes his reads:
    - ❏ O2 on the same-side sideline
    - ❏ O1 in the middle of the floor
    - ❏ O5 opposite sideline wide
    - ❏ O4 trailing

Player O4:

- If your personnel allows you to switch responsibilities, move O4 to the inbounder.

- After inbounding the ball to O3, steps in and acts as the reverse man and safety.

Player O5:

- Starts at the top of the key on the offensive end. Reads where the ball is inbounded and reacts by cutting up the floor opposite.

- Stays in that lane looking for the second pass, or keeps proper spacing as the ball is advanced.

INBOUNDS PASS TO O1

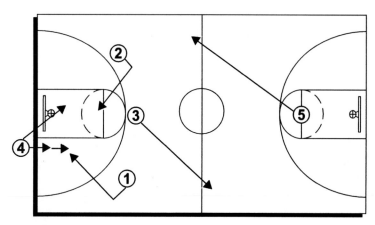

Figure 8-2

Player O1:

- Sets up his man and V-cuts to the ball. (See Figure 8-2.)

- As he catches the ball, makes the following reads:

  ❑ O3 making a diagonal cut in front of the ball to the same-side sideline

  ❑ O2 flashing to the middle of the floor

  ❑ O5 on the opposite sideline wide

  ❑ O4 acting as the reverse man

Player O2:

- As O1 catches the ball and O3 clears, flashes to the middle of the court for the second pass.

- If he gets the second pass, he looks to advance the ball by the dribbling.

Player O3:

- As the ball is inbounded to O1, makes a diagonal cut in front of the ball to the same-side sideline and remains on that sideline with proper spacing as the ball is advanced.

Player O4:

- Makes the inbounds pass to O1, then steps in and acts as the reverse man and safety.

Player O5:

- Starts at the top of the key on the offensive end of the floor and reads which side of the floor the ball is inbounded toward.

- Reacts by cutting to half-court on the opposite side of the floor wide to the sideline, opposite the direction of the pass.

INBOUNDS PASS TO O2

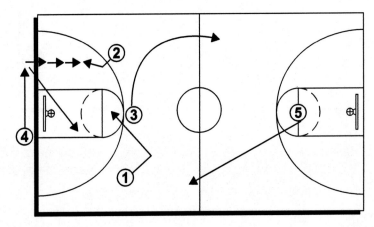

Figure 8-3

Player O1:

- Sees that the inbounds pass goes to O2, waits for O3 to clear, and flashes to the middle. (See Figure 8-3.)

- If he catches the second pass, he squares and looks to advance the ball with the dribble.

Player O2:

- Sets up his man and V-cuts to get open and receive the pass.

- Catches the ball and makes the following reads:
  - ❑ O3 on the diagonal cut in front of the ball to the same-side sideline
  - ❑ O1 flashing to the middle of the floor
  - ❑ O5 on the opposite sideline wide
  - ❑ O4 as the reverse man

Player O3:

- As soon as the ball is inbounded to O2, cuts diagonally in front of the ball on the same-side sideline and remains on that sideline with proper spacing as the ball advances.

Player O4:

- Inbounds the ball to O2 and steps in to be the reverse man and the safety.

Player O5:

- Starts at the top of the key on the offensive end and reads which side of the floor the ball is inbounded toward.

- Reacts by cutting up to half-court on the opposite side of the inbounds pass and stays in that lane with good spacing as the ball is advanced.

REVERSAL PASS TO O4

Try to always keep the three spots filled no matter where the ball is inbounded. Here's what to do if the ball cannot be advanced on the second pass and has to be reversed back to O4. (The beginning positions of the players in Figure 8-4 are where they would be after the first cuts on an inbounds pass to O3.)

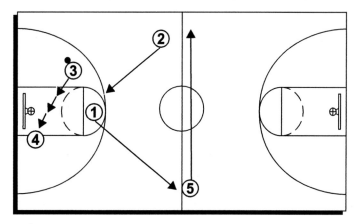

Figure 8-4

Player O1:

- As the ball gets reversed to O4, O1 cuts diagonally in front of the ball to the same-side sideline and remains in that lane as the ball is advanced up the floor.

Player O2:

- As the ball is reversed, O2 flashes into the middle of the floor as O1 clears.
- If he catches the second pass in the middle, he looks to advance the ball by the dribbling.

Player O3:

- After receiving the inbounds pass and O3 cannot find anyone open up the floor, he reverses the ball to O4 and becomes the reverse man and safety staying behind the ball.

Player O4:

- Catches the reversal and squares up with the following reads:
  - ❑ O5 on the same-side sideline wide
  - ❑ O1 making a diagonal cut in front and toward the same sideline
  - ❑ O2 flashing into the middle
  - ❑ O5 who has crossed the court
- Reverses the ball to O3 who has become the safety

Player O5:

- Looks for the immediate pass.
- As O4 receives the reversal and is covered, quickly crosses the court and positions himself sideline wide.

Summary

Some coaches like to have an auxiliary set of cuts, which the 3-up press breaker provides. However, you may use the same set of cuts used in 1-up and 2-up press breakers. The next chapter contributes drills to get the ball inbounds against face guard pressure and a set of drills to teach the *new* cuts of the 3-up press breaker.

You could even use the 3-up press breaker as your only press for the year. The cuts are basically the same, and a quick review of Chapter 5 will show you how these *new* cuts will break the most popular presses used today.

CHAPTER 9

Breakdown Drills for the 3-Up Press Breaker

B ecause all of the press breaker cuts are interchangeable, regardless of the initial formation (1-up, 2-up, or 3-up), it's easy to produce breakdown drills from the previous drills offered in this book. But two more are provided in this chapter to create even more challenging formations.

You can use the auxiliary cuts in the last chapter or the basic cuts from the previous chapters for your 3-up press breaker. Either way, it appears to be a new press offense that can throw off the defense. Your players have practically nothing new to learn while the defense must make major adjustments to keep you from inbounding the ball.

The 3-up and the 4-up (Presented in Chapter 10) formations create tremendous pressure on the matchup types of zone presses. But remember, regardless of the zone press being used, they all end, as does the double-teaming man-to-man press, in a trap, an umbrella, and a safety. Proper drilling against the trap and the umbrella allows your offense to see all types of presses.

Getting the ball in against denial pressure is the subject of the first drill (Figure 9-1). Once the ball is inbounded, continue practicing any of the cuts. Also, the defense can easily convert into a trap and an umbrella, representing all the major pressing defenses in basketball. Figure 9-1 illustrates O2 using the screen-and-roll with O3. Of course any of the three can screen-and-roll for another of the three, and you can devise signals for making such a call.

The second drill begins once the ball is inbounded (Figure 9-2). It shows the continuation of cuts every time the ball is reversed. This is especially important if you intend to use the press breaker to attack even half-court traps.

The beauty of using the same press against half-court traps is you don't have to learn a new system against half-court zone presses—just use the 3-up press breaker.

GETTING THE BALL INBOUNDS USING THE 3-UP PRESS BREAKER

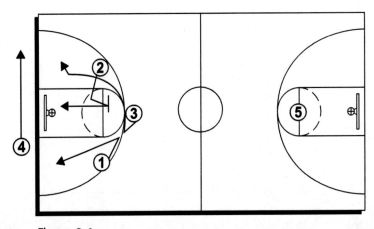

Figure 9-1

Procedure:

- Line up players as shown in Figure 9-1. Defenders are omitted so as not to clutter the figure, but X1 guards O1, X2 blankets O2, etc.

- X4 can play on the ball, covering O4 and trying to block his view of the inbound receivers. Or X4 can play shortstop on any of the 3-up attackers. X4 can even play center field.

- X1, X2, and X3 should deny their assignments the ball.

- Once the ball is inbounded, X4 can go trap with the inbounds receiver's defender. The other 2-up defenders can create the umbrella, and X5 can play safety. This gives the appearance of a zone press against the first pass.

- You can add X6 if you like to really make the offense work extra hard to break the press.

- O1, O2, and O3 can use individual cuts to free themselves for the inbounds pass.

- O1, O2, and O3 can even use the screen-and-roll maneuvers.

- If the defense intercepts a pass, they fast break.

- If the offense breaks the press, they fast break.

Objectives:

- To teach the offense how to get the ball in against denial pressure by both man-to-man and matchup-zone presses.

- To teach the offense the cuts after the first pass.

- To teach the offense to fast break once they break the press.

- To teach the offense to instantly convert to defense and stop the opponent's fast break after a turnover.

- To condition.

CONTINUOUS CUTS OFF REVERSAL OF THE BALL

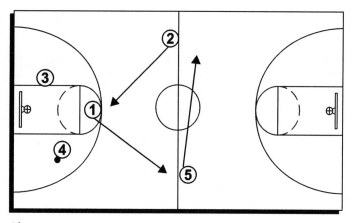

Figure 9-2

Procedure:

- Line up players as shown in Figure 9-2. Defenders are omitted so as not to clutter the figure, but again, X1 guards O1 and so on.

- X1, X2, and X5 face guard their assignments. X3 can play center field to keep O3 and O4 from throwing lob passes.
- You can even add X6 to do what X3 is doing while X4 and X3 double-team the ball when O4 has it or when O4 reverses the ball to O3.
- O4 has the ball. He checks the cuts of O1, O2, and O5.
- If O4 cannot hit any of the three cutters, he passes back to O3 who is the trailer and safety.
- O3 now checks O1, O2, and O5 as they run their cuts in reverse order.
- If the defense intercepts the pass, they fast break.
- If the offense breaks the press with their second pass, they fast break.

Objectives:

- To teach the cuts when the ball is reversed.
- To teach attacking the trap and the umbrella (both man-to-man and zone-press techniques).
- To teach the offense to instantly convert to defense when a turnover occurs.
- To teach the offense to fast break once they beat the press.
- To condition.

Summary

You now have another set of cuts if you prefer these to the previous set. You've even begun to develop an attack against half-court zone presses (See Figure 9-2).

You can use the tactics of the 3-up press breaker as a change-up in strategy to confuse even the most sophisticated types of defense (namely, the matchup-zone presses) without having to teach your players any new skills.

CHAPTER 10

4-Up Press Breaker

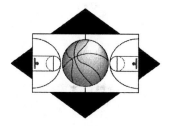

For the 4-up press breaker, four attackers are brought up to the free-throw line and extended area. This 4-up press breaker can be your only press breaker, or you can throw it into the mix as a strategic change-up. The entry pass can go to O4, O2, O1, or O5.

You can use the basic cuts presented in Chapter 3, as well as a few auxiliary cuts. You should determine which are best for your available personnel.

ENTRY PASS TO O4

Player O1:

- From his initial position on the elbow opposite the inbounder, O1 flashes to the middle of the floor as the pass goes to O4. (See Figure 10-1.)

- Remains in the middle lane asking for the ball as it is advanced. If he receives a pass, he attacks with the dribble.

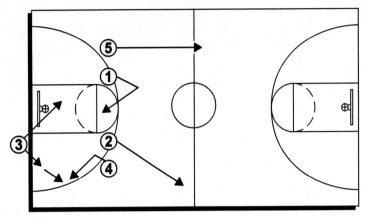

Figure 10-1

Player O2:

- As the ball is inbounded to O4, makes a diagonal cut to the same-side sideline.

- Remains in that lane as the ball is advanced.

Player O3:

- Inbounds the ball and steps in to be able to reverse the ball and be a safety.

Player O4:

- Sets up his man with a V-cut and squares up as he catches the ball and reads the floor:

  ❑ O2 on a diagonal cut in front of him

  ❑ O1 flashing to the middle of the floor

  ❑ O5 down the floor on the opposite sideline wide

  ❑ O3 for a reversal

Player O5:

- Fills the sideline wide at half-court.

ENTRY PASS TO O2

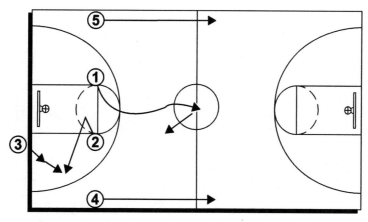

Figure 10-2

Player O1:

- As O2 receives the ball, O1 cuts diagonally in front of him to the middle of the floor, asking for the ball. If he does not receive the ball by the time he gets to half-court, he hooks back to help if needed. (See Figure 10-2.)

- Stays in the middle lane of the floor, looking to catch and advance with the dribble.

Player O2:

- Sets up his man and breaks for the ball.

- As he catches and squares, he makes his reads:

  - ❑ O4 filling the same-side sideline

  - ❑ O1 making a deep cut to the middle

  - ❑ O5 filling the opposite sideline wide

  - ❑ O3 for a reversal

Player O3:

- Inbounds the ball and positions himself for a reverse pass and to act as a safety.

Player O4:

- Fills the same sideline looking to receive and attack the basket.

Player O5:

- Fills the sideline wide position at half-court.

ENTRY PASS TO O1

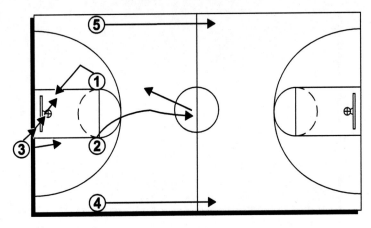

Figure 10-3

Player O1:

- Sets up his man and breaks to the ball. (See Figure 10-3.)
- As he catches and squares, he makes his reads:
  - ❏ O5 filling the lane on the same-side sideline
  - ❏ O2 making a deep cut to the middle of the floor
  - ❏ O4 filling the opposite-sideline wide
  - ❏ O3 for a reversal

Player O2:

- Makes a deep cut to the middle of the floor in front of O1. If he receives the ball, he attacks using the dribble.
- If he hasn't received the ball by half-court, he hooks back to help.

Player O3:

- Inbounds the ball and positions himself to be able to reverse the ball and act as a safety.

Player O4:

- Fills the sideline wide to half-court.

Player O5:

- Fills the same-side sideline looking for the second pass and staying in that lane.

ENTRY PASS TO O5

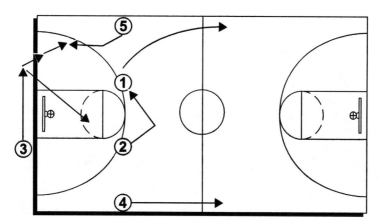

Figure 10-4

Player O1:

- Cuts diagonally in front of O5 after O5 has received the entry pass. (See Figure 10-4.)
- Stays on the same-side sideline looking for the second pass.

Player O2:

- Flashes to the middle of the floor asking for the ball. If he receives the pass, he advances the ball by dribbling.
- If he does not receive an immediate pass, stays in the middle lane, asking for the ball as it is advanced up the floor.

Player O3:

- Inbounds the ball by running the baseline and positions himself as the reverse man and safety.

Player O4:

- Fills the sideline-wide lane.

Player O5:

- Sets up his man as he sees O3 running the baseline and V-cuts to the ball.
- After catching and squaring, he makes his reads:
  - ❑ O1 diagonally cutting in front of him to the same-side sideline
  - ❑ O2 flashing to the middle of the floor
  - ❑ O4 moving down the floor and taking the sideline-wide lane
  - ❑ O3 positioned as the reverse man and safety

SUMMARY

You now have four new formations of press breakers, all using the same cuts. You can use them all interchangeably or decide to use only one set of cuts, but it's advisable to make use of two or three different formations.

The determining factor in any formation should be the personnel you have on hand. The individual drills in Chapter 1 can help your personnel improve on any press breaking deficiency they may have.

Your philosophy is important. Don't be content to just get the ball over half-court then set up your half-court attack. That type of thinking allows your opponents to press you all night and never have to pay for it.

The press breaker, whether you use the 1-up, the 2-up, the 3-up, or the 4-up, encourages you to attack your opponent's basket. Make them pay for extending their defense!

CHAPTER 11

Breakdown Drills for the 4-Up Press Breaker

The two drills in this chapter cover the two steps involved in breaking any press: getting the ball inbounds and then cutting to get open for the second pass.

The first drill is the 2-time screening maneuver. This commits all four of the up players to screen for one another and roll back to the ball. It doesn't matter which two players screen, as long as the entire team knows who is going to set the screen and who is going to accept the screen. Devise your own signals to call who screens for whom.

The second drill, posting up and slashing, is important from two aspects. It can get your best ball handler breaking down the middle of the court, easily giving you a fast-break basket, and it's an integral part of the attack against half-court traps. When you have a full-court press breaker that you can also use as a half-court press breaker, your players will know the offense more fully because they have less to learn.

2-TIME SCREENING MANEUVER

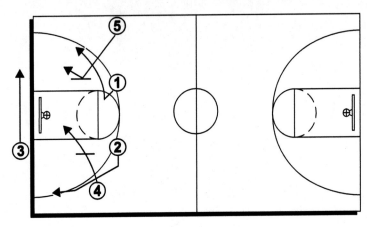

Figure 11-1

Procedure:

- Line up players as shown in Figure 11-1. Defenders are not shown so as to not clutter the figure, but X1 has O1, X2 guards O2, and so on.

- In Figure 11-1, O4 screens for O2 and rolls while O5 screens for O1 and rolls. But you could have O1 screening for O5 and rolling, and O2 screening for O4 and rolling. Or, you could have O4 and O5 making individual cuts while O1 and O2 operate the screen-and-roll.

- O3 runs the baseline. He reads X4 on the right side of the court and X5 on the left side of the court (Figure 11-1). If the defenders switch, O4 or O5 is the primary receiver. If the defenders do not switch, O1 or O2 is the primary receiver.

- You can allow X3 to play on the ball (on O3); you could put him at shortstop (double-teaming a particular receiver); or you could let him cover at the top of the key (center field).

- Once the ball is inbounded, X3 could double-team the receiver with the receiver's defender while the other three defenders create the trap and umbrella.

- The attackers who do not receive the inbounds pass must run their cuts off the first-pass series.

- If the defenders steal the pass, they fast break while the original offense tries to prevent the fast break.

- If the offense can break the press, they fast break to the other end of the court.

Objectives:

- To teach the screen-and-roll to get the ball inbounds.

- To teach the cuts of the press breaker.

- To teach O3 to recognize who the primary receivers will be.

- To teach the defense how to play denial defense into the trap and the umbrella (both a zone and a man-to-man press).

- To teach the defenders to fast break on a steal.

- To teach the offense to convert to defense rapidly and stop the opponent's fast break.

- To teach poise and control under pressure.

- To condition.

POSTING UP AND SLASHING

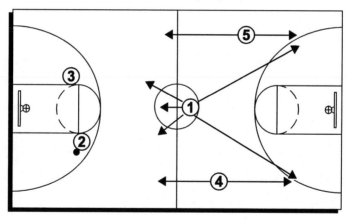

Figure 11-2

Procedure:

- Line up players as shown in Figure 11-2. Defenders are not shown so as not to clutter the figure, but X1 guards O1, X2 has O2, etc.

- O2 and O3 pass or dribble up the floor until the defense stops them.

- O1 tries to find an opening in the middle lane. If O1 gets a pass, he squares up and drives straight down the middle of the floor. O4 and O5 fill the wings on the fast break.

- If the pass went from O2 to O4, for example, O1 would cut diagonally toward the wing. If O4 can hit O1, O1 would dribble-drive toward the basket with O4 filling the middle lane and O5 the far-side lane. A lob pass is often available from O1 to O5 or from O1 to O4 to O5. O4 and O5 can help themselves get open on the sidelines by moving toward the end line before flashing back toward the ball.

- Defenders can be in a zone press or a man-to-man press, preferably the press of your next opponent.

- A steal by the defense should result in a fast break to the other end of the court. The offense must convert to defense immediately and stop the fast break.

Objectives:

- To teach the offense the cut of the 4-up press breaker.

- To teach how to attack the dropback, zone, and man-to-man presses.

- To teach how to attack the half-court zone traps.

- To teach O4 and O5 the V-cut to free themselves on the sidelines.

- To teach the defenders to fast break on a steal.

- To teach the offense to instantly convert to defense and stop their opponent's fast break.

- To condition.

Summary

These are only two of a myriad of drills you can devise to teach getting the ball inbounds and attacking off the first or the second pass. In the first drill, for example, you could allow O4 and O5 to use individual cuts and O1 to screen-and-roll with O2 to get the ball inbounds.

You could extend the second drill, for example, by allowing O2 to pass to O1, and O4 and O5 to slash toward the basket on diagonal cuts. Or, you could have O2 pass back to O3 and have O1 flash toward O3 to get the ball.

CHAPTER 12

Fast Breaking and the Secondary Part of the Press Breaker

A solid, strategic philosophy is to break the press with the first- or second-pass series and then take the ball hard to the basket on a three-lane fast break before the defense can recover making them pay for extending their defense down the floor.

This chapter is divided into four sections: the 3, the 2, the 1, and the 4 series.

When O3 throws the ball inbounds, he can often break the press with his first pass. The first three figures and explanations exhibit O3's first pass breaking the press, called the 3 series.

Most of the time O3 inbounds the ball to O2. He has three options on his second pass to break the press. This is called the 2 series.

When O2 is not open, O3 passes into O1, if possible. O1 has three passing options to break the press. This is called the 1 series.

When all else has failed, O3 passes into O4, who now has three passing options to break the press. This is called the 4 series.

All the series end in at least a three-lane fast break. Those lanes are pictured in each of the 12 figures in this chapter. If you don't get the fast-break lay-up or uncontested jump shot, you move into your secondary offense, which flows freely from the positioning after the fast break. It's the same secondary offense you run when fast breaking off steals, missed shots, or made shots.

THE 3 SERIES

O3's Pass to O5

Figure 12-1 illustrates O3's full-court pass to O5. This frequently occurs when X5 doesn't play safety well. It breaks the press immediately and provides for an easy fast-break lay-up or jump shot.

O3 passes to O5 (Figure 12-1). O1 cuts down the middle lane for a pass back from O5. O1 can drive all the way to the basket if that option is available. O4 fills the weakside sideline lane. O1 can pass to O4 for the lay-up or jump shot. If either O1 or O4 take the jump shot, O5 rebounds hard, if O5 takes the jump shot, O4 rebounds hard.

O3's Pass to O1

When O5 is not open and O2 cannot free himself for the inbounds pass, O1, as you may recall, must get open by an individual cutting move. When O1 receives this pass from O3 (Figure 12-2), O1 has the immediate option of dribbling the ball down the center lane. O4 would fill the weakside sideline lane and O5 would fill the strongside sideline lane.

This option to O1 is immediately open against a 1-2-1-1 zone press, and with proper cuts, O1 can easily free himself from man-to-man pressure.

O3's Pass to O4

If the defense is in a diamond-and-one, shading toward O1's side of the court, then O4 is immediately open. When all else fails, O4 must make a V-cut to free himself for the inbounds pass. Figure 12-3 illustrates O3 passing into O4. This is O1's cue to cut to the middle lane to receive a diagonal pass from O4. O1 continues with a dribble down the middle lane while O4 fills one sideline lane and O5 fills the other.

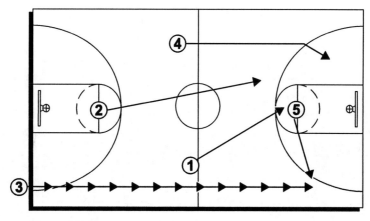

Figure 12-1

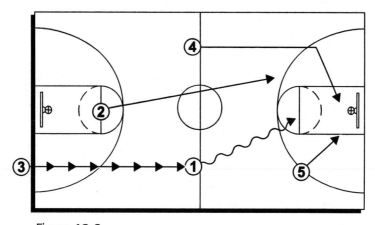

Figure 12-2

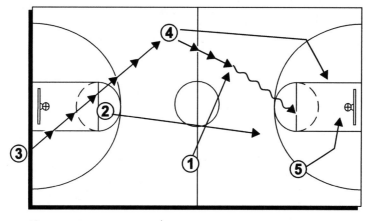

Figure 12-3

THE 2 SERIES

Figures 12-4, 12-5, and 12-6 begin with the ball already inbounded to O2 on the right side of the court. (If the ball were inbounded to O2 on the left side of the court, the cuts would simply change sides.) Figure 12-4 illustrates the pass from O2 to O5; Figure 12-5 illustrates the pass from O2 to O1; and Figure 12-6 illustrates O2's other option, a pass to O4. All end with the second-pass series of the press offense as presented in Chapter 3 (the first pass was the inbounds pass) breaking the press and ending in a three-lane fast break.

O2's Pass to O5

In Figure 12-4, O2 passes down the court to O5. When the pass was inbounded to O2, O4 flashed to the ball and O1 went crosscourt to the sideline away from the ball. This is a basic tenet of the press breaker. When the second pass went downcourt to O5, O1 broke back down the middle lane, and O4 filled the opposite sideline lane.

O2's Pass to O1

Figure 12-5 shows the second pass going from O2 to O1. 1 has the immediate option to begin driving the ball down the middle lane. O5's rule is to always go opposite the second pass putting O5 in perfect position to offensively rebound or fill the weakside sideline lane.

O1 has two options available once he receives the pass from O2 (Shown in Figure 12-5). O1, if it is available, begins to dribble down the middle lane. O2, once he passes the ball, runs the sideline deep cut. This puts O2 in perfect position to fill the right sideline lane. O4 breaks hard down the left sideline lane to fill that lane, freeing O5 to post and get the offensive rebound.

O1's other option is to pass the ball to O2 breaking down the right sideline lane. This option is not shown in Figure 12-5, but can be easily imagined. O2, if he receives the pass from O1, dribbles down the right sideline lane, O1 fills the middle lane, looking for a pass back from O2 if available. O4 and O5 would still do their weakside lane cuts.

O2's Pass to O4

As you may recall from Chapter 3, O4 flash pivots to the middle lane to give O2 a third possible attacking pass. O1's rule is to go to the weakside sideline and face the middle of the court in case O2 doesn't immediately hit O1 with the second pass.

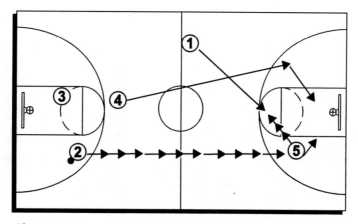

Figure 12-4

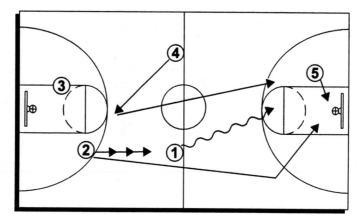

Figure 12-5

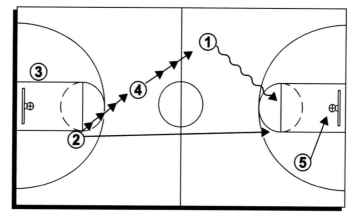

Figure 12-6

Figure 12-6 shows O2 passing to O4, O5 going opposite the second pass, and O1 setting himself on the weakside sideline lane. O4 then pivots, squares up, and passes to O1. This second pass could have bypassed O4 and gone directly to O1 if he had been open, and often he will be. In either case, O1 dribbles the ball to the middle of the court. O4 races to fill the left sideline lane, and O5 comes hard to the basket, filling the right sideline lane. After O2 makes the pass, O2 comes hard to the side of the key for a possible pass and a jump shot off the secondary break (subject of the book *Coaching Fast Break and Secondary Offense*). When your press breaker ends in your secondary break, just like your fast break does, your players have less to learn so they can execute their offense better.

THE 1 SERIES

O1's Pass to O5

Figure 12-7 illustrates O1 passing the ball to O5. O2 has already cut by O1 on a diagonal and gone to the left sideline lane to watch for his next option (Covered in Chapter 3). O2 now breaks to the middle lane looking for a pass from O5. O4, who flash pivoted, now sprints down the left sideline lane. O1 races hard down the floor and locates around the key for a possible return pass and a three-point shot.

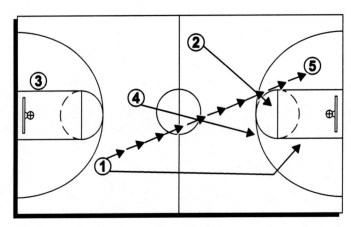

Figure 12-7

O1's Pass to O2

In Figure 12-8, O2 sees the inbounds pass from O3 to O1. This is O2's cue to make a diagonal cut. O1 passes to O2 as he cuts across the middle of the court or after he has cleared the middle of the court. This diagonal pass, as stated in Chapter 3, is almost impossible for a zone or man-to-man press to prevent. O2 dribbles the ball down the right sideline lane, O1 fills the middle lane, and O5, following his rule to always go opposite the second pass, goes to the right sideline lane. O4 races down floor to make himself available for the secondary break by positioning himself around the top of the key.

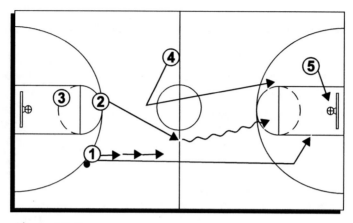

Figure 12-8

O1's Pass to 4

O4 learned in Chapter 3 to flash pivot whenever O1 receives the pass from O3 (Figure 12-9). O2, following his press-breaker rules, cuts diagonally by O1 for a possible pass from O1. When O2 does not get this pass, O2 cuts to the weakside sideline lane and looks for his second option. O1 now can pass to O4 who pivots, squares up, and passes to O2 who should be wide open against any zone or man-to-man press. O1, of course, could have bypassed the pass to O4 and passed directly to O2 if O2 appeared open. O5 follows his press-breaker rule and goes opposite the second pass. O2 dribbles the ball to the middle lane, O4 fills the left sideline lane, and O5 fills the right sideline lane. O1 races down the floor to make himself available at the side of the key for the secondary offense.

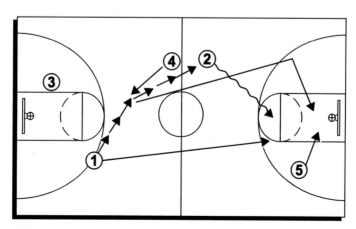

Figure 12-9

THE 4 SERIES

O4's Pass to O5

Figure 12-10 illustrates the long pass from O4 to O5. This frequently happens against zone presses. O5 should be taught to free himself for this possible pass against zone pressure. The opponent's safety in the zone press is usually the biggest and least mobile player. That's why O5 can often get himself open.

In Figure 12-10, O4 passes to O5. O1, who would have flash pivoted according to the press-breaker rules in Chapter 3, cuts to the right sideline lane. O1 could read the coverage and even take the middle lane if O2 could not get there in time, but O2 has been taught to go to the weakside sideline and await his next options. O2 cuts to the middle lane for a pass from O5, and the three-lane break develops. O4 races down the floor to get to the side of the key for the secondary part of the fast break.

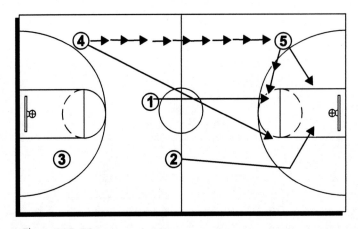

Figure 12-10

O4's Pass to O2

O2, according to this press breaker, cuts diagonally when he sees the pass going to O4. O2 intends to clear that side of the court if he doesn't get the pass from O4 (See Chapter 3 for these basic cuts). But in Figure 12-11, we are letting O4 hit O2 on this cut. O2 takes the ball to the middle lane on a dribble. O1, who should have flash pivoted per the press-breaker rules, will fill the left sideline lane. And O5, who always moves opposite the second pass, will be in perfect position to fill the right sideline lane. O4 races hard to the key area preparing for the secondary part of the fast break.

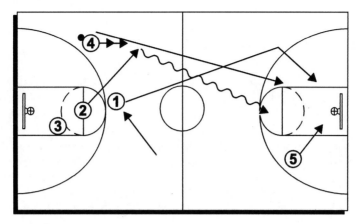

Figure 12-11

O4's Pass to O1

Figure 12-12 illustrates O4 passing to O1 who has posted up in the middle lane per his press-breaker rules (See Chapter 3). O4 could bypass this pass to O1 if he sees O2 is open on the right sideline lane. If O4 hits O1, O1 can take the ball on a dribble down the middle lane, or O1 can pivot, square up, and pass to O2 on the right sideline lane. Figure 12-2 illustrates the latter, the pass from O1 to O2. O2 now has the option of dribbling down the right sideline lane or dribbling the ball into the middle lane. O1 reads O2's decision. O1 fills the middle lane if O2 dribbles down the right sideline, or takes the right sideline lane if O2 dribbles to the middle lane. In either option, the three-lane fast break develops and the fourth player (O4 in Figure 12-2) races hard to the side of the key to position himself for the secondary part of the fast break.

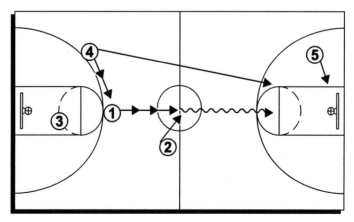

Figure 12-12

Summary

Each of these series ended in a three-lane fast break after breaking the press off the first or second pass series, which were fully discussed in Chapter 3. Each ended with a fourth player stationing himself near the side of the key waiting for the secondary part of the fast break to develop.

Notice that the best ball handler, O1 or O2, was always in charge of the ball at the end of the fast break. Also note that the biggest players were in position to rebound any missed shot, and in position to post up before the defense could get set.

O3 is always playing safety in case of a turnover; O3 also serves as a reversal of the ball position, meaning changing the side of the attack by reversing the ball.

You want the opponent to pay, and to pay dearly, for trying to press your players. Such an attitude develops aggressiveness, poise, control, and confidence in attacking any zone, matchup, or man-to-man press.

CHAPTER 13

Press Breakers Versus Half-Court Traps

This chapter will demonstrate how the press breaker works against half-court zone traps. It will present two patterns against an odd-zone trap and an even-zone trap.

When your full-court press breakers also work against half-court zone traps, it will reduce your teaching time and greatly increase your players' execution.

Figure 3-3 is expanded into Figures 13-1 and 13-3. This is, as you will recall, a basic tenet of the press breaker. Figure 3-3 illustrated O2 passing the ball into the flashing O4, and O1 rolling to the other side of the court. Figure 13-1 will illustrate how this simple maneuver can destroy the odd-front half-court zone trap; Figure 13-3 takes the same pattern (From Figure 3-3) and illustrates how it conquers the even-front half-court zone trap.

Then, we will take an auxiliary cut, Figure 8-4, and illustrate how it is expanded to shatter the odd-front half-court zone trap (Figure 13-2) and the even-front half-court zone trap (Figure 13-4). From these explanations, you can easily see how all the other basic cuts and auxiliary cuts will work against the half-court zone traps. You merely need to choose which patterns you want to teach for any particular year. Choose the ones most compatible with your current personnel.

This chapter will be divided into two sections: Attack Versus Odd-Front Half-court Zone Traps and Attack Versus Even-Front Half-court Zone Traps. Each section describes the most popular zone traps to attack—1-2-2 for the odd front, and 2-2-1 for the even front.

ATTACK VERSUS ODD-FRONT HALF-COURT ZONE TRAP

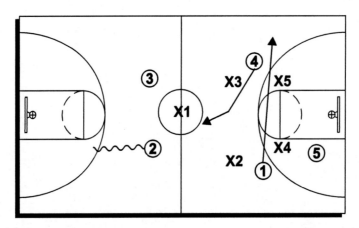

Figure 13-1

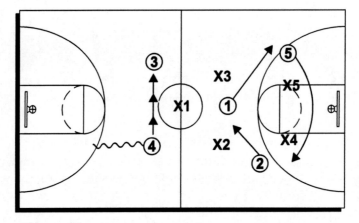

Figure 13-2

Figure 13-1 expands Figure 3-3 into a half-court zone trap attack. It is a continuation of a basic 1-up cut. Figure 13-2 elaborates Figure 8-4 into a half-court zone trap attack.

Basic Cut

With no pressure in the backcourt, but seeing the half-court trap in front of him, O2 dribbles the ball toward midcourt but does not cross the half-court line (Figure 13-1). O3 trails O2 for the reversal pass and to act as safety.

X1 and X2 cannot go trap immediately. If they did that, then either O1, O3, or O4 would be left wide open for an easy pass that would break the purpose of the half-court zone trap. If O1 or O4 were left open, it would result in a three-lane fast break.

O4 times his cut into the middle lane for a pass from O2. O1 has cut across the court to the weakside sideline lane, per his press-breaker rule: *same side cross, opposite side middle.* O5 can run the baseline, but begins on the same side as O2, per his press-breaker rule.

The odd-front zone trap cannot cover these cuts. X2 must guard his space for fear of a pass to O1; or when O1 vacates, a pass to O5 cutting up from the baseline (Figure 13-1). X3 must cover the cut to the middle of the court by O4. But if X3 covers this cut, then no one is covering an overhead-flip pass to O1 on the left sideline. X5 cannot come away from the basket to get O1 because that would give a lay-up opportunity to a cutting O5.

Several fast-break options are available. O2 could pass to O4, who takes the ball down the middle lane on a dribble. O2 could pass to O4, who passes to O1, who takes the ball along the left sideline. Or O2 could pass to O4, who pivots, squares, and if covered by X5, passes low to the cutting O1.

If O2 does not see that O4 is open, then O2 passes back to the trailing O3, who can immediately dribble the ball into the frontcourt. Or, O3 can make a quick pass to O1 on the right sideline, because X3 had to take the center-lane, flash-pivot cut of O4 and cannot possibly get back to cover the passing lane to O1.

Auxiliary Cut

O4 and O3 are bringing the ball down the floor, per the auxiliary cut of Figure 8-4. O4 dribbles up to half-court but does not cross the line. O3 is the trailer and acts as safety, per the press-breaker rules.

Figure 13-2 illustrates O1 already in the middle lane. He must be initially covered by X3, or a pass from O4 to O1 will give O1 the driving middle lane with a dribble. This leaves an overhead-flip pass to O5 open, unless X5 vacates the basket area and comes to cover O5. O5 can receive this pass from O4, immediately pass to O1, and the break is on.

X1 and X2 cannot go trap O4 immediately. That would leave O3 open for an easy pass and dribble, which would break the half-court zone trap. Neither could X1 and X3 go trap immediately because that leaves O2 open for an easy pass and the three-lane fast break. Do not be afraid to allow O4, one of your bigger players, to handle the ball.

If X2 comes to put some pressure on O4, then O2 is open. If X4 comes high to cover O2, then no defender is near the basket. When this occurs, O5 should cut behind the last line of defense, compelling X4 and X5 to retreat near the basket.

Figure 13-2 illustrates a reversal pass from O4 to O3. O5 pauses a moment in case O3 drives toward the middle and makes the pass to O5, or if available, makes a quick touch pass to O5 after receiving the pass from O4. It's impossible for X3 to cover both the middle lane and the quick pass down the left sideline lane.

As the pass goes from O4 to 3, O1 immediately cuts to the left sideline lane, and O2 follows O1's cut into the middle lane. Meanwhile, O5 has rolled beneath the last line of defense and momentarily posted himself on the right low-block (Figure 13-2). A pass from O3 to O2 would see O2 pivoting, squaring, and dumping low to O5 for a lay-up. A pass from O3 to O1 would see O1 passing to O2 cutting down the middle lane, driving down the left sideline lane, or tossing a lob pass to O5 for the lay-up.

ATTACK VERSUS EVEN-FRONT HALF-COURT ZONE TRAPS

Basic Cut

Figure 13-3 is an extension of Figure 3-3 and follows the rule: *same side cross, opposite side middle*. O5 is on the same side of the ball per his cutting rule off the first pass.

X1 has O2, and X2 has O3. O3 is the trailer and safety. X3 begins on O1, but X3 ends up guarding space when O1 cuts crosscourt to the opposite sideline lane. X3, however, must cover his space, otherwise, O5 would break high for the pass that breaks the half-court trap (Figure 13-3).

X1 and X2 cannot go trap immediately. If they did, then either O1, O3, or O4 would be left wide open for an easy pass that would break the purpose of the half-court zone trap. If O1 or O4 were left open, it would result in a three-lane fast break.

When O4 cuts to the middle lane, X4 must follow and deny O4 the ball or the press is broken. But if X4 denies O4 the pass, who can cover O1? If X5 comes up to cover O1, O5 receives the pass and lays the ball in the basket.

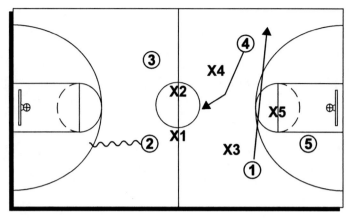

Figure 13-3

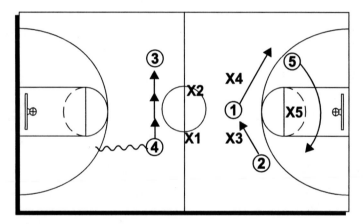

Figure 13-4

A pass from O2 to O4 sees O4 dribbling down the center lane, and a three-lane fast break results. Or, O4 can receive the pass from O2, pivot, square up, and pass to O1 on the left sideline. O1, who is your best dribbler, attacks the basket with a dribble. O1 now can pass to O4 cutting down the middle lane for a slam dunk or throw a lob pass to O5 cutting on the far side of the basket, depending on how X5 tries to stop the fast break.

Auxiliary Cut

Figure 13-4 illustrates an auxiliary cut attacking the even-front half-court zone trap. (Figure 13-4 is Figure 8-4 expanded.)

O4 has the ball dribbling down to but not crossing the half-court line. O3 is trailing per his press-breaker rule. O1 is stationed in the middle lane, posting up (Figure 13-4).

O2 and O5 are behind X3 and X4, compelling those defenders to stay at home in their coverage. But if they stay home, who has O1? Either X3 or X4 has to come up to cover O1, or X2 has to drop off O3 and cover O1. Because O5 is farthest away from the ball and O4 has the ball, X5 will probably come up to cover O1. If this happens, O5 is open for an overhead-flip pass from O4. Then O5 can touch pass to O1 cutting down the middle lane, and a three-lane fast break occurs.

X1 and X2 cannot go trap O4 immediately. That would leave O3 open for an easy pass and dribble, which would break the half-court zone trap. Neither could X1 and X3 go trap immediately because that would leave O2 open for an easy pass and the three-lane fast break. Do not be afraid to allow O4, one of your bigger players, to handle the ball.

If the defense decides to play it safe and let X2 drop to the middle lane to cover O1, then the reversal pass to O3 results in O3 driving the ball across the midcourt line, or passing to O1 who is cutting. O3 can, as he drives into frontcourt, passes the ball to O2 in the middle lane. O2 pivots, squares up, and passes to O5 who cuts behind the last line of defense for a lay-up. Or O2 can dribble down the middle lane for a three-lane fast break. Or, if O3 passed to O1, O1 can bring the ball down the left sideline lane for a three-lane fast break.

You can easily see a half-court zone trap, whether odd-front or even-front, is no match for press breakers.

CONCLUSION

In this book, you were presented a simple, easy-to-teach press breaker, with eight basic options and several auxiliary cuts. You were even given the press breaker from four formations: 1-up, 2-up, 3-up, and 4-up. You only have to use one, if that's your choice, or you can use more than one. There's very little extra to teach once you have mastered any of the four formations, and it's worth learning all of them because an added formation can thoroughly confuse even the best of defenses.

Each of these progressions has a first-pass series and a second-pass series. You need both because sometimes your players will not see the openings. Both the first- and second-pass series have three outlet-pass lanes, a must for attacking great pressing defenses.

You have a myriad of breakdown drills to choose from so you won't have to run your entire press offense every day in practice. You can drill only the aspect you feel needs extra work.

Also, vital drills were given in the first chapter that you should use even if you don't choose any of the press breakers. Those drills will improve all your individual players in their efforts to attack pressure.

Finally, if you use this press breaker, you already have an attack against half-court zone traps without having to teach anything new.

ABOUT THE AUTHOR

Bob Huggins is a proven success as a program-builder, recruiter, game-strategist, and motivator. He has demonstrated this in a variety of ways since joining the University of Cincinnati in 1989.

Inheriting a team that was short on numbers, Huggins inspired his initial team to a postseason tournament and has done so every year since. Coach Huggins has compiled an impressive 332-100 record in his first 13 years at Cincinnati, making him the winningest coach in U. C. history.

For his efforts, Coach Huggins has been awarded many coaching honors, including the Ray Meyer Award as the Conference USA Coach of the Year in 1997-98, 1998-99, and 1999-2000. He was also Basketball Times' selection for national coach of the year in 1997-98.

Huggins began his coaching career as a graduate assistant at his alma mater, the University of West Virginia, in 1977. Subsequent coaching stints have included Ohio State (1978-80), Walsh College (1980-83), Central Florida (1983), and the University of Akron (1984-89).

Born in Morgantown, West Virginia, Huggins grew up in Gnadenhutten, Ohio where he played high school basketball for his father, Charles Huggins, at Gnadenhutten Indian Valley South. Bob and his wife, June, have two daughters, Jenna and Jacqueline.